When
God
Becomes
Small

"Reading *When God Becomes Small* is like making a quiet walk through a fruit-laden orchard at harvesttime. The pages here, like the limbs and branches there, are hung with sustenance and truth; and at almost every turn of the path or the page, there is that perfect sentence that startles with its insight and its economy of expression. This is a gentle book, a quiet book, a very ripe and informing book. Savor it."
— Phyllis Tickle, author, *The Words of Jesus: A Gospel of the Sayings of Our Lord*

"*When God Becomes Small* is an encouraging, amazing, helpful book that is well written, and among the very best books I have read. It sings with a spirit of poetry, wisdom, and hope. This book will stir in your life the blessings of God's generosity and grace. After reading it, your life will be richer and fuller."
— Kennon L. Callahan, researcher, professor, pastor, and author of twenty best-selling books.

"In a world that proclaims that 'bigger is better,' pressing us toward acquisition and ladder-climbing, Phil Needham gently reminds us of the gospel's refreshing countermessage. *When God Becomes Small* invites us to enter into the freedom Jesus offers. When we follow his path—setting aside glory and embracing the humble—we discover God's shining presence in the smallest things: the lost coin, the tiny mustard seed, the invisible child, and even our own lives."
— Christine Chakoian, senior pastor, First Presbyterian Church, Lake Forest, IL

"The need to think freshly about God is a desire in many of us. We need a guide on this journey, for considering anew our understanding of and life with God is not for the faint of heart. Phil Needham is a uniquely qualified guide on this journey. With wisdom born from age, insight born from struggle, sincerity born from love of people, Phil has given us a gift in this exceptional book. It is ideal for all who have a deep sense that there is more to God than we have thought, dreamed or imagined."
— Doug Pagitt, author, goodness conspirator, and pastor of Soloman's Porch

"In a mixture of intimacy and distance, Phil Needham has presented God in a way so becoming that some of us will want to start over."
— Fred Craddock, legendary homiletician, author, and director of The Craddock Center

When
God
Becomes
Small

Phil Needham
(in association with Crest Books)

Abingdon Press
Nashville

WHEN GOD BECOMES SMALL

Library of Congress Cataloging-in-Publication Data

Needham, Phil, 1940–
    When God becomes small / Phil Needham.
        pages   cm
    ISBN 978-1-4267-7871-1 (pbk. : alk. paper)   1. Humility—Religious Aspects—Christianity.   2. Christian life.   I. Title.
    BV4647.H8N44 2014
    231.7—dc23

                                                                          2013035392

14 15 16 17 18 19 20 21 22 23—10 9 8 7 6 5 4 3 2 1
MANUFACTURED IN THE UNITED STATES OF AMERICA

To Keitha, my wife of fifty years,
who sees beauty in small things, finds grace in unexpected places,
and makes music wherever she goes.

Contents

Acknowledgments

BOOKS WOULD NOT BE POSSIBLE without the generous and insightful help of others. This is one of them. While I alone take full responsibility for these pages and any flaws they contain, they are better than they would have been without the support and wisdom of family and friends.

My wife, Keitha, has made two important contributions. As the draft of each chapter was completed she made excellent suggestions. She also granted me the hours of privacy needed to complete the book. For Keitha, a highly interactive person for whom social engagement is life itself, this was both a gift and a personal sacrifice. My sister, Miriam, and her close friend, Robin, also read the chapters as I completed them and offered valuable suggestions.

Friend and mentor Ken Callahan has been a wise and reliable guide for me over many years, beginning with a class he taught at Candler School of Theology, Emory University, back in the 1970s. Over the course of the ensuing years, I have had the privilege again and again to seek his counsel and draw from his wisdom. His comments and stylistic suggestions, as well as his probing challenges, have made this a better book.

Editors Constance Stella and Jennifer Manley Rogers have brought considerable clarity to what I have tried to accomplish. Their wisdom has been invaluable, and their critical eye helped me improve the book by both sharpening certain passages and pruning verbiage.

Preface

THIS IS A BOOK WRITTEN FOR two types of people. It is for people who long to experience the God who is promised by their own faith—a God who is engaged in our lives, who enlivens our relationships with the people around us, and who ignites our compassion and empowers us to respond to the needs of this world. Many people recognize a discrepancy between the God of their beliefs and the God they experience, or want to experience, or perhaps cannot experience.

This book is also for people who are drawn to the idea of a close and personal God but who have yet to see strong evidence that such a God exists. For many, the most compelling evidence seems to point in the opposite direction. And so, life hums along. But now and then we wonder, and even wish.

We wish for a God who is worth believing in, who is close enough to meet us where we are. We are perplexed by the emptiness of the world and our human accomplishments, and we have had enough of our own oversized drives and cravings. We are tired of striving without satisfaction and searching without finding.

My hope is that as you engage this book, the skies may clear a little, bringing in new light and a few surprises. My hope is that you may see God, and perhaps yourself, in a new way.

part 1

The Seduction
of Bigness
and
The Hunger
for Smallness

One

Our Obsessing Over More
and
Despising of Less

WE WAKE UP ONE MORNING, restless about where we are in life, dissatisfied with ourselves. We wonder where we can go from here, what more we can do to satisfy our longings or get more out of life. Our dissatisfaction may be rooted in a salary we think is too small, a home we think too humble, a marriage that is not as fulfilling as we had hoped—or something else we imagine is the cause of our discontent.

We look around and see people who seem to have more than us, or better lives than us, and it strikes us as unfair—even wrong. We could look deeper and search our souls. We could allow ourselves to see the gifts of God already at our fingertips. But our attention is drawn instead to what others have and we don't, and we covet it.

What accounts for this? Why do we want to be more than we

are and have more than we have? Why this craving to be better than the next person, in one way or another—more respected, better looking, more successful, more prosperous, more ethical, more holy, more talented, more honored, more erudite, or more "together"? What are we really grasping after here? And why?

I suspect that on some level what we seek is significance, a recognition of our worth and acknowledgment that our life has value. No one wants to be a lesser person or, far worse, a nobody. So we desperately seek some form of self-enhancement, hoping it will give us significance.

In a materialistic society, this desperate search for significance leads to an all-consuming pursuit of wealth. In the world of marketing, record sales. In the world of politics and sports, winning. In the academic world, being published. In the world of entertainment, becoming a media idol. In the world of the church, having one of the largest and fastest-growing congregations. In the world of our personal faith, receiving recognition of our admirable devotion to matters of the Spirit. This obsession with more tempts us every direction we turn.

How Jesus Sees It

If we study the teaching of Jesus of Nazareth, we are shocked to learn that he gives no positive acknowledgment of such attainments as markers of genuine significance. Quite the contrary: He warns against their deceptive seduction. Wealth easily distracts the mind and consumes the heart. Success tempts us sorely to think more highly of ourselves than we ought, positioning us for a fall. The adulation of fans and admirers tricks us into a dangerous lack of self-awareness. The drive to succeed and be admired as a church leader cloaks an arrogance no less deplorable for the religious language and coating.

If we study the life of Jesus, we are shocked even more by his disdain of wealth, status, adulation, and fame. He's born dirt poor and chooses to stay that way. He spends his time almost exclusively with the poor and marginalized; people of status have to impose upon Jesus, or make an appointment with him during off hours, or arrest him in order to have a conversation. When people, after seeing his messianic charisma and miraculous power, try to get him to lead a rebellion against the Roman occupiers, he slips away. He orders people not to publicize his works and increase his fame. He remains in the relative obscurity of Palestine for almost his entire life. And frankly, he shows little or no deference for people in high positions, secular or religious; in fact, what he says about them usually brings them down a few notches.

If we want to take Jesus seriously, we must come to terms with his opposition to our obsession with more and bigger claims. And we must see the true Jesus beyond the Jesus we've dressed in the values of our grasping, success-driven culture.

A helpful place to begin is to understand how we have come to embrace so fully the moral shallowness of a culture that wants "more and bigger for *me*." How has this seduction grown to have such a grip on us? What lures us to strive for the top and define our significance by position, power, or possessions? And how does this seduction distance us from God?

A Mindset of Scarcity

The overriding assumption supporting this drive to the top, to have more and to be better than others, is the mindset of scarcity. It is a mindset that assumes there is never enough for everyone, and we always need more. There is never enough food, never enough money, never enough resources to make us secure, never enough positions of prominence, never enough respect to go around.

The result is a deep dissatisfaction with what we have, and this creates a desperate desire for what someone else has. If there is not enough to go around, I will probably want what you have. World empires are built because nations believe they must have more land, resources, and influence. Some corporations exist solelyto acquire other corporations and assets to increase their market share, wealth, and prominence. The addict lives in continual fear there won't be enough of whatever it is that he or she craves and overindulges when the fix is available, whether it's alcohol, drugs, food, work, power, or some other hit. Churches and denominations compete for market share of potential new members, as if there were not enough people to go around. If we believe there is never enough, we think we always must have more.

It seems clear this is the conclusion at which we have arrived. We believe we are too insignificant, too small, and therefore we must expand our reach in a world of limited opportunity. We think our worth is measured by our position on some scale of comparative value, whether the scale is power, wealth, status, fame, influence, respect, social prominence, moral uprightness, or ideological purity. What drives us is to be higher or the highest on the particular scale or scales we use to measure our personal value. We define our lives by these scales of our choice, and we measure our success— indeed, even our significance—by how high we think we are on those scales. As a result, life becomes a race to the top, and seeing so many below us is our security and perhaps even our secret pleasure. There is nothing wrong with the drive to exel, but Jesus warns us to take a hard look at the scales of value we use. As he said to the high achieving Pharisees, "What is highly valued by people is deeply offensive to God" (Luke 16:15b). This ought to give us all pause.

What we inevitably discover is that the higher we go and the bigger we become in these ways, the more we weigh ourselves down and incapacitate ourselves for a life journey that is actually worth taking. Hopefully, we begin to suspect life is not an accumulation of the rewards and recognitions of our success. We may even uncover a surprise: our letting go of these things brings us closer to the real substance and significance of life. As Jesus said, "He who loses his life will save it" (Luke 9:24).

Holding tight to a "never enough" worldview means believing, down deep, that neither God nor anyone else will provide for your needs. Never enough breeds suspicion and fear. It either leads to a preemptive strike or to a resigned paralysis. We grasp for power and position or we give in to our helplessness. When buying into the mindset of scarcity, we remove ourselves from its opposite: the abundance of grace. By letting go of such desperation, we open ourselves to the possibility of discovering a gracious God we can trust, a God who cares for us and is there for us.

A Limited Shelf Life

The pursuit of bigness results in a heavy investment in things that are temporary and cannot last. It is similar to stockpiling items with expiration dates on shelves. To use a metaphor of Jesus, it is like storing grain in bigger and bigger barns only to have the grain spoil over time, useless to anyone.

World empires eventually become unwieldy and unsustainable and collapse. Huge business conglomerates become overly complex, lose their focus and their edge, and begin to sell off more and more assets in order to survive; and if they do not reinvent themselves into a leaner and refocused enterprise, they slowly fade away or go bankrupt. Megachurches are in danger of succumbing to the hubris of their success, and without their rediscovery of humility and refocus on a mission outside themselves, they are eventually left vacant. Anyone with a high public profile can lose it overnight because of shifting landscapes in public tastes, political power, new ideologies, or personal moral failure.

For all human beings, the thought of losing whatever status, power, or prominence achieved thus far in life is frightening. Jesus predicts the downfall of prominent religious leaders in Jerusalem, along with the destruction of their temple, the central symbol and presumed enduring monument of their religious authority. The shelf life of their strong position in the community was about to expire. The threat of losing their status was enough to frighten the leaders into forming a plot to have Jesus killed (Matthew 23, 24).

People will fight like cornered lions to save the influence and leverage they have earned, inherited, or had conferred upon them. The intensity of their desperation is a measure of how important to their own self-worth their now-jeopardized position is. If and when there is little of real value left after such a position is gone, desperation and fear ensue.

We can see this in the life of Judas Iscariot, one of Jesus' disciples. Judas misreads the intention of Jesus' mission and therefore his own position in a new order. He interprets the revolutionary role of his leader as the overthrow of the Roman oppressors and the reestablishment of a Jewish state. This view of Jesus' role places priority on who holds the power and grants privileges. I recently saw Judas's extreme disappointment over the failure of his high hopes portrayed in the famous Oberammergau Passion Play by Weisand and Daisenbergh. In one scene Judas confronts Jesus with Jesus' failure to set up a political kingdom:

> "Why should I still follow you?" he says. "Your great deeds offered hope that you would restore the realm of Israel. But it has turned to nothing. You are not grasping the opportunities that offer themselves to you....I want to share your reign. But it fails to materialize." (2010, 27–28)

In truth, the kingdom of heaven is materializing before Judas's eyes. He doesn't see it because he has given in to the lure of an expanding kingdom built on power and promising him a place of recognition and prominence. Being robbed of this possibility makes him susceptible to fear and desperation. He turns Jesus over to the authorities, either to force Jesus' hand to lead a political revolution or to protect himself in the aftermath of its failure.

Had Jesus led a revolution of the kind Judas wanted and had it succeeded, it would have had a limited shelf life. The shelf life of the existing order was protected for the time being, but it, too, would last only four more decades. The powerful Roman Empire that destroyed it also had a limited shelf life. Weakened from within by the complacency and arrogance of its own success, it would eventually crumble under the duress of new invasions. And so it has gone throughout the course of human history. No power-based empire lasts. The search for bigger and better leads to a dead end where the search can go no further and life is no more.

Despising Small Things

The world Jesus invites us to enter is the world of small things. He describes lilies as more gloriously adorned than the robe of King Solomon (Luke 12:27). He speaks of the importance of a housewife finding a small, lost coin and holding a house party to celebrate (Luke 15:8-9). He says any shepherd worth his salt will not only leave his flock of ninety-nine sheep to find one lonely stray but will also throw a party to celebrate the rescue (Luke 15:4-6). Jesus honors and celebrates the little things.

Our current society honors and celebrates the big things. In retail, sales need to be bigger. In manufacturing, profit margins and output need to be bigger. If you're on the company board, stock returns need to be bigger. If you lead a church, attendance and membership need to be bigger. If you're a parent, your child's achievements need to be bigger. Our world honors and celebrates these accomplishments in a myriad of ways, reinforcing the priority to be big.

Protests can be mounted against an addiction to more and

bigger, and rightly so. Fortunately, there are exceptions to living a life chained to the addiction to bigger, there are people who are not dazzzled and enthralled by bigger or more. They have a refreshing simplicity, a deeper relationship with fewer things and a real intimacy with people. They celebrate their connection with life, not their greater accomplishments. In this sense they are aligned with a down-to-earth Jesus.

Most of us acknowledge it is emotionally healthy to invest ourselves in the simple things in life. We also know it is morally right to have concern for marginalized people. It is further true that our drive toward power and prominence can threaten these values and push them down further on the scale of priorities.

I do not write this because I question the motives or values of people who are successful merchants, business people, CEOs, church leaders, or the parents of high-achieving children. I write it to draw attention to an ethos that permeates our culture. I have deep respect for highly successful people, many of whom possess a profound humility, whose personal integrity and concern for others are important keys to achieving their success—individuals who are more concerned with how their success can benefit the lives of other people, especially those who are disadvantaged, than they are with indulging a lust for personal prominence. They are distinguished by their departure from the operative norm.

What is it that saves some from the arrogance of bigness and the despising of "small" people and "lesser" things? This is actually a question for all of us, because any of us can be seduced by the pursuit of bigness. If we haven't yet achieved bigness, we can pursue it through our dreams. We can long for the day when our ship will come in. Or, we can be wedded to the belief that hard work will eventually make us rise to a level of recognized success because, as one founding father of our country said, "God always helps those who help themselves." Any of us can be lured into the lie that success is salvation and more is better. This book invites you to see in a different way.

Means Becoming Ends

An important step toward this freedom is to understand how the drive to the top has necessitated a value system and success measurements that major in lesser matters. In our day I think we largely measure success by elevating secondary matters to greater prominence and treating more substantive matters as incidental. Or, naively, perhaps cynically, we are claiming substantial outcomes result when we succeed in the lesser matters. We convert means into ends, intermediate goals to final goals. We assign more value to accomplishments easily measured than to substantive, life-changing outcomes that don't fit easily into standardized measurements.

I can easily illustrate this with the community most associated with my own vocation: the church. It makes sense for a congregation to measure such things as attendance, membership, and budget. These are one dimension of assessment. But they do not finally tell us if that particular congregation is living the life and accomplishing the mission to which its founder, Jesus, calls all his disciples. More people in attendance may mean little more than the success of attractive programs and the high entertainment value of services. Membership increases may mean little more than the successful recruitment to a religious club of like-minded people at, possibly, the exclusion of other people who, because they are different, make the club members uneasy. Expanded budgets may mean little more than good fundraising techniques and expanded membership of people with financial resources. None of these alone proves that the congregation is discovering and modeling the life and mission of radical compassion, inclusive outreach, and spiritual depth to which the church of Jesus is called. In fact, as we all know, a congregation deemed successful by the standards of attendance, membership, and budget has sometimes proved to be self-centered, self-serving, and self-promoting—a congregation compulsively driven in their pursuit of more and bigger.

The same kind of dynamic where efficient means take

precedence over, or even replace, substantive ends can happen with any group of people, as well as individuals. It happens wherever growth in size, power, money and profits, status, or enhancement of profile and respect trump both the group's or company's original mission and its regard and concern for its constituencies. In the case of a manufacturer, for example, how highly are its employees regarded and its customers respected?

A Christian who embarks on a spiritual growth plan may think and hope that simply performing certain actions and disciplines will deliver greater emotional health and spiritual maturity. He or she may think the means, of themselves, will deliver the ends. Having followed the prescribed actions and disciplines, he now considers himself to be spiritually mature. Or she convinces herself the means have delivered the ends. In reality, the means may have delivered only activity, and he or she may have only deluded and indulged the self. The true ends have much more to do with the person coming to terms with an inner journey and a real calling as a compassionate disciple of Jesus.

In all situations where in one way or another means become ends, secondary things become primary, there is a diminishing of our humanity. We quantify and measure ourselves in order to feel better about our progress and our worth. We quantify people and treat them as enhancers of ourselves—as statistics, objects, factors, consumers who can add to our benefit and enlargement. Having substituted means as ends, we see people as numbers to attract, recruit, manipulate, and even exploit. We transform them into building blocks in our own empires and consumer goods meant only to meet our own needs, and in doing so we also transform ourselves into power-grabbers and egoists who define our worth quantitatively, and our relationships by how much the other person props up our own self-esteem and recognition.

The obsessing over more and the despising of less leads us to a dehumanized and dehumanizing world—one where we all become exploiters who must deny the full humanity of those we exploit, including ourselves. This is usually done in subtle ways, often with plenty of kindness. The evolution of terminology used to describe a company's employees is one example of diminishing personhood: once employees were personnel, then they became human resources, and finally human capital (Norris 2008, 123). The pursuit of bigness finally leaves us dehumanized, and when all is said and done, diminished. We lose sight of each other, and our overextended lives feel more and more like empty shells. God has a different way. He invites us to get small and find the true beauty and value of who we really are.

Two

The New Attraction to Small

JULIE PENNINGTON-RUSSELL is senior pastor of a large church in Decatur, Georgia. Upon approaching her fiftieth birthday, she decided she would celebrate by climbing nearby Stone Mountain fifty times over the course of the year. In an *Atlanta Journal-Constitution* guest column, she said the first lesson she learned from the experience was the enormous value of "feeling small" (2011, A21). As she stood on the top of this huge granite mountain that predated her by millions of years, a kind of liberation came, a liberation from the tendency to oversize the issues and matters of her life and, at the same time, to embrace the deep significance of her small place in God's bigger picture.

A Small World, After All

My wife, Keitha, and I live in a home on a small lake in a neighborhood that borders a huge county park surrounded by thick forest. As we are officially retired, we spend a good deal of time at home, and much of that time is occupied with observing the world in our backyard. Our last few placements with The Salvation Army involved a considerable investment of time and energy in matters relating to the mission effectiveness of the organization. During that busy period, we had to work hard to nurture and protect our more intimate relationships and our times of personal reflection. Now that we are retired, we can more fully experience the pleasure of our smallness in the captivating world that is close by.

Our backyard is a fascinating place where fish thrive in our little lake and heron and kingfishers catch them; geese and ducks come and go and one pair usually nests; deer, foxes, coyotes, otters, beavers, and muskrats visit; squirrels and chipmunks appear regularly and snakes occasionally; lake turtles and snapping turtles appear every day, save in the cold winter; and frogs croon during the summer nights. Indeed, our backyard is a very small world full of wonder.

Keitha has a special affinity for the birds. She puts out a variety of seeds and suet regularly. There is a pecking order in our backyard café. The woodpeckers top the order, followed by blue jays and brown thrashers, then doves, cardinals, and robins, the various finches and sparrows, and finally the chickadees. The smallest ones seem so overpowered, but they cleverly take advantage of every opening and play an important role in the avian order. I'm told the little chickadees typically give first warning to the other birds when a hawk is approaching.

In his poem "The Oven Bird," Robert Frost wrote, "The question that he frames in all but words is what to make of a diminished thing" (1969). Frost knows the oven bird speaks to us both through his wordless song and in his silence, "a diminished thing" calling us from our distraction with bigger things to hear a more enduring voice. Part of the penetrating genius of this great American poet was his ability to observe the small things around him and see in them profound truth and startling revelation. We learn from Frost that small things can be more than minor distractions; they can be doorways to deeper meaning.

The Hunger for Small

No wonder we see signs of a renewed interest in small things: our civilization has exhausted itself with overload and overreach. This trend was observed by Rich Rodriguez in a *Los Angeles Times* article titled "Future Shock: The Bigger We Feel, the Smaller We Want to Be" (2000, M1). Rodriguez stated it in a paradox: "Never have Americans had so many reasons to feel themselves gigantic upon the earth; never have so many Americans wanted to feel themselves dwarfed on the earth."

Our telescopes are peering into infinity, our technology promises us the world (and beyond), online retailing puts just about everything at our fingertips. A recent TV ad is built around an astounding claim: "I have the right to be unlimited!" Billionaires are considered the smart ones. Larger-than-life Hollywood and sports celebrities are the ones who matter, otherwise we wouldn't follow their lives so eagerly. Hype and gossip overrule thoughtfulness and insight. Partial truth is expanded to create a big and convincing distortion, which is what most news programs have largely become.

This obsession with the high and the mighty, the big stories, the expansive empires, and the cultural icons whose power over us is godlike, has left us with a longing for something we've missed. Rodriquez calls it "a hunger for small."

Down to Earth

There is another way small things connect us with larger reality. We remember important events that have huge implications beyond our private worlds by connecting them with related small details in our personal lives. I was too young to have any memory of the day Pearl Harbor was bombed, but my parents could tell you where they were and what they were doing, as well as how this event affected them over time. I can, however, remember the day World War II ended. My family lived in New Orleans, and I was four years old. The sounds of church bells and car horns still ring in my ears, and the sight of people shouting and sometimes dancing in the streets is a memory that has never left me. I can tell you where I was and what I was doing on the days President Kennedy and Martin Luther King Jr. were assassinated. It's as if these momentous events require specific associations and connections with our smaller world, our own place on earth, in order to be grasped and felt.

In her fictional autobiography, *A Tree Grows in Brooklyn*, writer Betty Smith reveals a way to give personal significance to larger events. She describes how Francie (the character in the story who represents the author) intentionally follows the advice of Granma Mary Rommely: "To look at everything always as though you were seeing it either for the first or last time: Thus is your time on earth filled with glory" (1943, 390). On the day the United States enters World War I, Francie collects small items reminding her of that specific day, including the very first newspaper clipping on the story, and puts them in an envelope. Because the war is so much bigger than her life, it is important that she make it small with concrete memories to which she can relate. Years later, when she is leaving her office job to go to college, she mostly spends her last day in the office taking in every detail, snapping vivid mental photographs. Her last office break time includes gathering around the piano and singing the songs she and her colleagues loved most, songs that will help keep her connected with the bittersweet memories of those years. All these concrete memories help Francie frame a huge transition she never imagined would be possible for her: entering college to become a writer (1943, 389). A last day in the office remembered in detail, brought down to familiar earth, gives reality to what is probably the most momentous turning point in her life.

So too for us, the small details give concreteness and texture to larger events in our lives, the full significance of which we may not grasp at the time. In fact, to rob these events of their detail and see them only in terms of meaning tears them from the fabric of our story and makes abstractions of our lives. I love to get together with my siblings (two brothers and a sister) and retell the stories of our growing-up years together. It's the details, over which we sometimes disagree, that make the stories palpably real. (I suspect our disagreements over details signal our good-natured sibling rivalry for ownership of the stories.) Keitha does the same with her three brothers, but, miraculously, all four seem to agree on just about every detail. I enjoy listening to their stories even though I've heard most of them many times over. The fact of the matter is this: The smaller details of our stories are what give life to the journey. Without them, our lives would be lifeless, a story not worth telling, and certainly not as interesting.

Treasuring Small Things

I love the story Kathleen Norris tells in *Acedia: A Marriage, Monks, and a Writer's Life* about her three-year-old niece. The girl's father would drive her to day care in the morning on the way to work, and her mother would pick her up on the way home. Often the mother would peel an orange and bring it to her daughter when she picked her up. One day Norris came across her niece playing "Mommy's office" on the front porch of their home. She asked her niece what her mommy (a stockbroker and financial planner) did at work. "Without hesitation, and with a conviction

I relish to this day," says Norris, "she looked up at me and said, 'She makes oranges'" (2008, 216).

There you have it. The real significance we have for each other, the things that connect us at the deepest levels, are found not so much in the appeal of our stature, influence, and accomplishments as in the attraction of small graces and specific kindnesses. The active vocational lives Keitha and I pursued kept us very busy advancing an organization's mission and addressing numerous personnel and administrative matters associated with it. In our retirement, we have more time and energy to be attentive to small things. We have come to realize that the small things really are the big things—they are the profound and cherished. In fact, we are convinced that the contribution any of us makes to the lives of other people has much more to do with small graces and personal attentiveness than with large accomplishments and professional advancement. We've tested this by remembering what incidents or experiences with certain people most impacted us. There may have been some large accomplishments on their part that impressed us; but what affected us most deeply was their interest in people, including us, and the ways they made themselves available to us. It was their simple grace and kindness that told us they cared. It was their ability to get small and connect.

When we measure the value of our lives solely by such accomplishments as how far our career advanced, how high a position we reached, how much power we wielded, how much adulation and how many awards we received, or how much we influenced the course of events, we have missed what will give us the only real satisfaction at the end: the enduring treasures of intimate relationships, love expressed, mercy given, encouragement offered, gifts shared—these are like oranges a mother must surely spend all her day making for the one she loves. Life must surely be as small, and as large, as that.

Facing Our Pursuit of More

If the small things actually are the most lasting and meaningful, why, then, are we continually impressed by those who achieve high positions, enormous power and influence, or large-scale recognition? And why do we wish we were they? What is the force by which they seduce us to covet what they have and call it significance?

I believe our attraction to more and bigger is fed by our *fear*— our fear of being overwhelmed and getting lost as the world we live in expands at a rapid pace. Our fear of being left behind in the competition we wrongfully see life to be. Our fear of not having enough and therefore always needing more, and more, and more. Our fear of not being loved or liked unless we measure up, or build up, or climb up. Our fear of each other. Our fear of God, if we believe in him. Fear is the subtle and unrecognized demon that drives us to doubt our adequacy and distrust our relationships. It lures us to find worth in what we accomplish rather than in who we are. It tempts us to live a driven life in which each new accomplishment is never enough because the demon of fear keeps haunting us with our inadequacy.

Fear is the enemy of relationships. Nothing is more hurtful than broken relationships, hatred thrown in our face, not being valued or even recognized by another person, inability to share our hearts with someone we love, and embarrassment when we try but fail. Trusting relationships then become more difficult because we fear the hurt and rejection. Intimacy is now a threat. As we become increasingly uncomfortable in our small world of relationships, we see the larger world as a viable escape from intimacy and larger pursuits as alternative sources of affirmation. The lonely person often becomes the driven person.

There is good news. It is hidden in our growing disillusionment with what bigger and better actually delivers. This drivenness that favors our hubris over our humanity proves to be no compensation for our loss of intimacy. This may encourage us to suspect there is a better way. Perhaps, however, our fear still will not allow us to stop. In desperation we try harder, and harder, but to no avail. We can't seem to shake the self-doubt, the lingering sense of our inadequacy. No matter what we accomplish, it is not enough to fulfill us. No wonder many now question the American Dream. Either we fail in realizing the promise of prosperity and wealth, or having realized it, we find our spirits starved.

What if there was a very different dream worth living, one that nourishes our spirit? I believe there is. And what if it was already available to us? I believe it is. This dream invites us to take a journey to explore our own hearts, share our lives with those nearby, and then pour more of our energy into quiet compassion outside our family circle. I believe the real treasure is to be found not in the far-away of some recognized empire we build but in the more intimate world of our backyard, our common life. I strongly suspect this is true both for the person who is known only by his small circle of family and friends and for the high-profile person who is known by tens of thousands.

It is not that a drive toward expansion has no inherent value; it may well have the potential to add value to our society. Much good has been done on large scales, and even enterprises undertaken successfully for self-serving reasons can also benefit others. What diminishes us as persons is investing our lives in larger pursuits without investing significantly in deep relationships. What robs our souls of the gift of caring is to fail to see the human faces of those around us and of those affected by what we do.

It is time to face up to our fear of each other, come down to earth, and look into each other's hearts. It is time for human accessibility. It is time for close, informal relationships that give the rich color and texture of grace. It is time to turn aside from our obsession with big, bigger, and biggest so that we can have space to risk getting small with each other. The reward of that risk is to be able to love another and be loved, and to share love with an ever-widening circle of persons. Surprisingly, one of the biggest barriers to human intimacy is a distorted view of God.

part 2

Distorted
Beliefs in
God's Greatness
and
How He
Invalidates Them

Three

The Great, Inaccessible God

LET ME INTRODUCE YOU to my childhood religion. In my earliest years I saw God as a kind of cosmic father figure. He was not mean or cruel, but he did live a long way away, and he did have rules I was supposed to live by. For the most part, I did live by them, and when I didn't, my main punishment was guilt. (I used to envy my older brother who I thought got away with murder and somehow seemed to have an exemption from the curse of guilt.) Despite the discomfort of that occasional weight of guilt for my failures, my "religion" seemed to be working pretty well for me during those years. My childhood was secure and largely satisfying.

Jesus was in the picture, too, and whereas he seemed much more accessible than the cosmic father figure, I saw him as a kind of harmless, gentle person who walked around a storybook Palestine and said nice things to nice people (especially children) and sometimes harsh things to deserving, sinful people. I was able to identify with the nice people, so long as I didn't slip up and commit some kind of transgression. When I did slip up, I knew how to work the system as I had been taught. I brought my feelings of guilt to Jesus, who somehow then made things right again with the heavenly Father. This penitential routine worked relatively well for me during those childhood years. I was not only given some relief from my guilt but also extrinsically motivated toward a certain goodness.

There were two things about it all, however, that satisfied neither my heart nor my mind as I matured during the teen years. One was my sense of the remoteness and inaccessibility of God. Why was there so much distance between us? Was God's "greatness" so great that he was always beyond me, so perfect that I, imperfect as I was, had no hope of a relationship with him? Distance and differentness tend to foster suspicion, just as intimacy and connectedness tend to lead to trust. A distant God is a God to be either feared or doubted. Since doubting was not an option in my childhood religion, thoughts of God the Father sometimes unsettled me.

The other dissatisfaction was my confusion about Jesus. This gentle Jesus meek and mild was a needed alternative to the all-powerful deity, but I saw his goodness and kindness as so incredibly perfect as to put him beyond mere humanness. I had trouble seeing him as a real human being. He was, as it were, the good and gracious side of God, the side I found it more difficult to see in the God of heaven. Perhaps I can sum up my emerging dilemma in this way: it was hard to reconcile the great and all-powerful God with the sensitive, caring rabbi called Jesus, who was also supposed to be the same God.

In the next chapter we will deal with how Jesus of Nazareth actually brings God down, close to us. For now, I want to describe how many people are still caught up in (we might even say hold themselves captive to) this idea of a great, inaccessible God, the divine father figure who gives rules rather than a relationship.

Indeed, some carry this childhood Christianity into their adult years, unable to grow beyond it. Unlike the Apostle Paul who, when he became a man allowed himself to put away childhood thoughts and replace them with radically new understanding (I Corinthians 13:11-12), some cannot let go of their conviction of God's remoteness. The second thing I want to explore in this chapter are the ways we compensate for a God who seems so distant and inaccessible as to be, for all intents and purposes, absent. If we feel God is so far away and hard to please, then what do we believe? How do we live?

First, let us consider how God became so remote to our way of thinking. A helpful place to begin is to identify how two very different views of God met each other and what the outcome has been.

Two Views of God

Christianity did not spring up in a cultural vacuum. Jesus was a Palestinian Jew, and his first disciples practiced their faith within Jewish culture and religious ritual. Within a relatively short period of time, however, his followers began to infiltrate the Gentile (non-Jewish) world. Largely through the cross-cultural boldness of the Apostle Paul and other early Christian heroes, the faith was planted in the hearts and minds of people across the Mediterranean world. The protected travel routes of the powerful Roman Empire and the courage and evangelical passion of those first missionaries combined to make it possible for Christianity to become a Mediterranean-world religion.

Birthed from Judaism, Christianity considered Jewish scripture as its own. In those writings Christians found a God like the one described in Isaiah's temple vision, "sitting on a high and exalted throne" (Isaiah 6:1). But they also found a God who came close enough to speak to people, either directly (as with Abraham and Moses) or through prophets. They also found metaphors of God as a shepherd watching for the safety and health of his sheep (Psalm 23), or as a lover longing for reunion with his beloved but unfaithful people (Hosea). And most startling of all, the first Christians found the first book of this Old Testament saying that this "high and exalted" God created humans in his own image (Genesis 1:26-27). God was indeed great, but his greatness did not make him inaccessible to us, nor did it make us totally unlike him.

When Christian missionaries entered the larger Mediterranean world, they found a multitude of ethnicities, each with its own religious views and regional gods, but the glue that seemed to hold together this otherwise confusing diversity of outlooks together was the intellectual dominance of the great Greek philosophers. Chief among those whose writings wielded significant influence was Plato. The god of Plato was ideal perfection, the supreme soul within whom there could be no variance, no differences, no change of any kind, and therefore no emotions. This was a god whose perfection allowed no interaction with human imperfection.

It would be hard to imagine a greater contrast than that between this god of Plato and the God of the Old Testament. Israel's God was portrayed as a person with extremes of emotion (tenderness and anger, for example), as an active participant in Israel's life, as a force to be reckoned with, and as an intervening rescuer of his beloved people. One need only read King David's song of deliverance recorded in I Samuel 22 (preserved in Psalm 18, as well) to see that Israel's God was no distant unmoved mover; he was a real presence and an interested participant. The New Testament takes this a huge step further in its witness to God's Incarnation (meaning "becoming a human") in Jesus of Nazareth. This understanding is in stark contrast to the idea of Plato's supreme soul for whom becoming a human would be logically absurd.

In order to win the war of the minds, however, many Christian theologians decided they had to engage Plato and his disciples on their own turf. The Christian creeds beginning in the fourth century actually use some of the language and concepts of Plato and the Platonists. One could arguably say this was necessary in order to communicate Christian faith in the thought forms of the day. Lurking behind such strategies, however, is always the possibility that this other way of thinking could actually change something essential to the faith being communicated or explained. The fact is that, at least in the Western Christian church where the influence of Plato has been persistent to this day, God has often been seen as distant and different from us, unchangeable, otherworldly, a consummate concept more than a feeling person— closer to Plato's view than that of the surprisingly intimate and "human" God of the Old and New Testaments. This idea of a remote, immovable God lingers to this day, both in some Christian theology and in the minds of many Christians. It lingers in my memory of my childhood faith.

Why would we hold to this view of an invariable God, a God who does not change his mind, a God whose greatness makes him inaccessible? What does it do for us? Ironically, it gives us a way to control him, or so we think. Having boxed him into his state of unchangeableness, we think we can predict him. We say God is consistent, so we can figure him out (Lord, just show me the rules, and I'll live by them). Or we say he is remote, so we can ignore him (the Lord won't notice; he doesn't really care how I live); or we may even dismiss him (God is only a projection of our minds, a desperate attempt to fill the gap of our knowledge and answer questions we don't yet have good answers to). This unmoved mover–God is not someone you would spend time with; a heavenly legislator who issues clearly defined laws that we always must be so careful to obey does not sound like a source of deep joy. We would think to stay clear of him, which is, in fact, what most do. And it would be an easy next step to disprove his existence, or at least doubt it, which some also do.

A *Questionable Greatness*

God is the victim of the questionable greatness we have ascribed to him. Indeed, God is great, but I fear we have missed his true greatness, and in so doing we have distorted and sometimes undermined the stunning truth of the Christian gospel. God is not great because he is high above us or remote from us; he is great because he is the Creator who constantly and compassionately takes the risk of interacting with his creation. What better place for the Apostle Paul to say this than in the presence of Greek philosophers gathered on the Areopagus, where the brightest minds in Athens debated each other (Acts 17:16-28)! Having identified an altar dedicated to "an unknown God," which I imagine some of the philosophers may have associated with Plato's supreme soul, Paul startles them by claiming, first, that this god is actually the one God his gospel proclaims and, second, that this God "isn't far away from any of us." Forget remoteness, deal with presence, says Paul. Forget ignoring or dismissing God, consider the joy (and at times discomfort) of knowing him.

Another interesting claim Paul makes in his message that day is that God's greatness is not at all measured by how different he is from us. His emphasis is quite the opposite: he quotes some of Greece's own philosophers by saying we are God's offspring. Of course this is a metaphor, not to be taken literally, but it does point to a very close connection between God and us, who are created in his image. In some of his letters, Paul is also fond of calling us God's children and God's sons (includes women). And at one point he appeals to our human nature in likeness to God by inviting a congregation to "imitate God like dearly loved children" (Ephesians 5:1). These words assume the intimacy between parents and children where both a capacity for likeness and the possibility of learning the family's way of life are assumed. Such a way of thinking makes no sense without the reality of a natural affinity between God and humans, as damaged as the relationship itself may have become. The greatness of God is enhanced when we actually show some credible resemblance to him, not when we bear little to none.

My childhood faith gave me a God of questionable greatness. I felt his remoteness. I was a speck of dust in the whole scheme of things. Fortunately, I was surrounded by family and other loved ones who gave me a very different sense of who I was. As we affirmed and sometimes fought each other, I gained a sense of my identity. I learned both to love and to be strong. What I discovered as the years progressed was that God was as close to me as these significant persons in my life. In fact, he often loved me, spoke to me, and fought with me through them. As time moved on I also discovered and encountered him in many unexpected places. Sometimes, it was a pleasant experience, sometimes confrontational. Usually, it was up close and personal.

There are still times when God seems remote and inaccessible to me. These may be times when, for whatever reason, I doubt myself, which becomes a way of pushing God away, the very one who does *not* doubt me. Or these may be times when God is withdrawing himself and forcing me to experience his absence in preparation for knowing his presence in a new (and better) way. This is a good absence, something worth waiting through as disturbing as the emptiness may be, because of what follows it.

For so many, it seems the sense of an absent God is *not* worth waiting through. It is unsettling, unacceptable. They decide God must be *made* present in some form or another. They conceive of him in ways that make sense to them, and then worship the god they have fashioned to assure themselves. They get on with a proper, comforting religion. I imagine we have all done this at one time or other—fashioned a god that made us feel at peace.

Whether we experience God as absent or as inaccessible, we are left with the same dilemma of his perceived remoteness. And so we compensate by reinterpreting who God is. Left to our own devices we make him in *our* image, reversing the truth of who we humans are. We compensate for our unfortunate captivity to the conviction of God's inaccessibility by making lesser gods, who then endorse what we project on them. God is shrunk into this lesser god who matches our tastes and sanctifies our ambitions.

No wonder our world is in a mess. We have created multiple little gods, each one endorsing and blessing our competing interests, dividing us into our private worlds with our own private deities. Meanwhile the continuing myth of the inaccessible God robs us of understanding that the one God, Creator of us all, actually "isn't far away from any of us" and holds the key to our true identity and deep joy (Acts17:27b). We do not have to make him in our own image. But we do. Consider now the profile of these gods who are compensation for our loss.

Our Compensation: Lesser Gods

There are many lesser gods, but they all share this in common: we do not serve them. They serve us. We envision them as accommodating to our narrow-minded religion and our private comfort. We may refer to our lesser god as the Christian God and even believe strongly, or innocently, that he is. Wanting to put our minds at rest that we are good Christians, we allow ourselves to believe that God is as narrow as our self-centered lives wish him to be, his values correspond with our own, and his purposes align with ours.

Such an attitude is idolatry: the worship of a lesser god, a god (by whatever name) created in our image, a god who serves our own misguided purposes. This idolatry can take many different forms, from the seemingly harmless religious underpinnings of a very respectable social group to the blatant religious endorsement of violence toward people who are not like us. It is easy to identify and condemn the latter extreme. We know the Nazis sang "God is with us" and convinced many people that God loved Aryans and hated Jews; and we know that much cruel terrorism is carried out as an obedience to some god who hates and commands his followers to destroy the infidels. It is more difficult to see and name the idolatry of nice people whose god favors their particular values, security, and lifestyle. The ugliness is usually not revealed until those things are threatened, questioned, and exposed as a desperate exclusivism. Respectable people can turn violent, even though their violence is usually delegated.

The lesser gods do not necessarily endorse violence towards outsiders, but they always endorse and sanctify obsessive self-centeredness. Indeed, the lesser gods are projections of the lusts and addictions to which many have surrendered. They apply a spiritual respectability and even virtue to drives that are, underneath, nakedly self-serving and may even involve the exploitation of others.

Consider the lesser god of *power and position*. This god subtly convinces us our worth is measured by these very terms and not by the value given us by our Creator. We are valued by how high we rise in the economic order or how widely we are able to force outcomes, whether the realm of operation is church, business, government, or some other organization or community. Blessed are those who rise to the top; unfortunate are the powerless nobodies. Such a conviction is unacceptably crass and insensitive when stated, but it is all the more pervasive and powerful for its hiddenness and for the subtlety of its influence.

It is not true that power *always* corrupts, but it does seem many fall prey to the corruption. We are no longer surprised when we learn of someone in a position of power being caught using that power for inappropriate, self-serving ends. Sometimes a person shows him or herself to be corrupt from the start, obsessed with accumulating power and achieving high position from the very beginning of his or her adult life. Perhaps more tragic are those who begin humbly but over time fail to resist the seduction. When the priest Samuel chooses Saul as Israel's first king, he demurs and cites his lack of qualifications. He finally accepts the position of considerable power, but with hesitation. Over time, however, the power goes to his head and corrupts his heart, and his life comes to a tragic end.

The Bible does not hesitate to tell many such stories, as if to drive home the point that becoming enamored of the lesser god of power and position is an abandonment of the true God and a demeaning of both oneself and others. Near the end of his earthly life, Jesus the powerless prophet from the insignificant town of Nazareth stands before the institutional power of both national religious leaders and governing authority. For a short time their power prevails, but it does not take long for the earthly powerlessness of Jesus to launch a movement that laughs at earthly power and then goes on to draw people in by the power of love.

Consider the lesser god of *wealth*. This god compensates for our disconnection from the living God by offering the accumulation of assets and luxuries as a pleasing distraction from spiritual depth. It is no accident that, in the Gospels, Jesus says far more about money than he does about prayer. He knows the dangers of money. At one point he tells a rich man to sell what he has and give the money to the poor. This otherwise righteous man goes away sad. Then Jesus says, "It's easier for a camel to squeeze through the eye of a needle than for a rich man to enter God's kingdom" (Mark 10:17-25). Jesus points to the folly of wealth accumulation in a parable about a man who keeps building more and more barns to store the grain he grows. Hoarding gives him a great sense of security—until the day comes for him to account for his life, and the wealth proves a total loss (Luke 12:13-21).

The Declaration of Independence speaks of the right of every person to the pursuit of happiness. Historian Diarmaid MacCulloch notes we have the Greek philosopher Epicurus to thank for the idea that the pursuit of happiness is life's ultimate goal. What the Declaration of Independence omits, says MacCulloch, is Epicurus's original qualification that happiness consists in the attainment of inner tranquility (2010, 40). In the minds of many Americans, the pursuit of happiness is associated with material acquisition, as if this pursuit could only be the accumulation of wealth. In other words, successful capitalist enterprise is the way that promises happiness. Pursuing wealth as a path to happiness, however, is a dead-end street that leads nowhere worth going. It is only a desperate substitute for spiritual wealth found in what is already nearby, and in the next acquisition. It is only the lie of a lesser god.

The lesser gods are many, and they all offer bigger and better. They are not only power, position, and wealth but the lesser gods of legalism, ideology, physical beauty, sex, drugs, and other obsessions. If we believe God is so distant he doesn't matter or that he doesn't exist, we are left to find one or more of these lesser gods that will invite us into their promise of self-enhancement and ultimate happiness, a promise on which they cannot deliver. The lesser gods are no more than our compensations for the God we think we have lost. The other kind of compensation is not self-enhancement; it is self-belittlement.

Our Compensation: A Lesser Human

If God is too distant to be involved in our lives, then we are too far removed from him to reflect his nature. We are trapped in a state of dark ignorance by God's absence.

That is exactly how many of the intellectual descendants of Plato saw the human situation in the century following Christ. Certain Christian thinkers tried to blend the Christian God with Aristotle's unmoved mover in complex schemes of thought we refer to as *gnosticism*. The word comes from the Greek word *gnosis*, which means "knowledge." One could move closer and closer to

God through progressive steps of acquired spiritual and mystical knowledge, eventually achieving full union with God. The part Christ played in these schemes was to come as the emissary of God and bring the needed gnosis to those who were prepared to receive it. This salvation plan was so complicated and esoteric, only the more educated and elite classes could participate. The poor and uneducated were excluded.

Central to gnostic teaching was the conviction that humans are souls trapped in evil bodies. The human soul was seen as the divine part of the person, and the journey toward union with God required a progressive freeing of the soul from the evil influence of the body and all things material. Those who did not qualify for this journey of enlightenment (the great majority) had little to no hope for salvation. Gnosticism consigned them to spiritual inferiority.

In one form or another, gnosticism is still with us. We see it in the person who bases the authenticity of his or her Christianity on the correctness of doctrine. Such a person considers he or she has the secret of saving truth because he or she believes the right things. It is this esoteric knowledge, this *gnosis*, that saves him or her. This person places hope in what he or she knows rather than in how he or she lives. It is quite possible that while this Christian concentrates on getting his or her mind right, he or she will fail in getting living right. Jesus said, "I came so that they could have *life*—indeed, so that they could live life to the fullest" (John 10:10, emphasis added). He did not say, I have come to impart doctrines. Jesus came to change our lives. The problem with gnostics of every ilk and age is that they miss the main thing Jesus was interested in: the radical transformation of people.

The other problem with gnostics is their pessimism about human nature. In one form or another, they believe our situation in this life is largely hopeless. Unlike the earlier gnostics they may believe that God actually did create the material world, but they see this world as having been taken over by evil, thereby reducing it to a kind of satanic kingdom. In this life humans are trapped within an evil world, and our souls are trapped within an evil body. The only hope is in an afterlife where we are freed from the inescapable corruption.

How then does the one who sees this world as essentially evil live in it? There are two possible choices. The first is that he can hunker down and invest enormous energy in suppressing and fleeing all carnal temptations. A life of this kind may be admirable, and even if it is fairly successful in its execution, there is little or no room for joy in it. Does a true and living God want those he loves to live this way? Is he making us work hard for the fullness of life he wants for us? The irony of this approach to the present life is that the suppressing and the ongoing flight from carnality keeps us focused on who we are *not* rather than who we *are*. Is this any way to live?

The second possible choice is based on the view that our sinful physical nature is so impossible to change in the present life that we must invest only in bringing our souls closer to God. Our bodies are corrupt, but if we have the *gnosis* it does not matter how we treat them or what we do with them, nor does it matter how we relate to the material world. Gnostics can then dismiss their own bodily indulgence and materialistic pursuit as insignificant play that cannot affect their souls. They see the grace of God as a cosmic indulgence that ignores sins of the flesh on the part of those whose souls are being purified. The purification is presumably unaffected by the sins. The sins may be confessed on a regular basis, but that is all that is needed. One could almost say, "Let us sin that grace may abound!"

What is clear is that gnosticism, in any form in which it appears, gives scant prospect for fulfillment in the present world. Gnostics live either in joyless suppression of material enjoyment or in undisciplined indulgence of it. Both lead to an emptiness of spirit and an absence of deep joy.

We humans are not just souls who happen to be imprisoned

temporarily in worthless bodies. We are embodied souls. We are not lesser humans on this earth waiting for a disembodied eternity, though many think we are. Our bodies are essential to our being and identity, and the world is the environment in which God has graciously placed us. As citizens of God's world, we bear his image and by his grace can claim this identity and begin to live out our true humanity.

The world is the place where God meets us. However, if we see God as far away and too big for us, this world becomes a place of darkness and despair. If we falsely ascribe to him a high-and-away greatness and make him untouchable and untouching, we are left on earth as lost souls, desperately seeking the long way back to him.

The Seduction of Our Smallness

Giving God a false greatness and placing him in a distant location also helps to excuse our smallness. Seeing ourselves as abandoned or trapped helps open the way to our personal downgrading. If we are small, we need not expect much of ourselves. God's forgiveness, assuming we think we actually need it, should be expected. How could he not extend it to those he has abandoned? How can I be blamed for my sins? "I'm only human" becomes our mantra of acquittal.

Beneath the mantra, however, is a disturbance, a bothering word, perhaps an inkling of our insincerity. It may be silent and muffled or loud and clear, but it is the word telling us who we really are and objecting to the claim of our pathetic smallness. It says we do not preserve God's greatness by making ourselves small. Our lack of courage and our tolerance of human weakness and exploitation do not make God look bigger and better. They are an insult.

We may cultivate a certain honesty about how small people can be. We may become astute observers and commentators of human behavior, pointing out the flaws, inconsistencies, scandals, and depravities of those around us. The question is: Do we apply the same searing observations when looking at ourselves? Or do we see ourselves as flawless, aiming the criticism only toward others? It is always difficult to see any unflattering reality about ourselves, to see our own frailties.

With some people, however, this is not the case. They have been so belittled and abused that they have come to accept the lie of their insignificance and the state of their victimization. Children who have been labeled as worthless, stupid, ugly, or sinful all too often carry that image of themselves into and even throughout adulthood. Children and adults who have been abused and used in one way or another find it hard to escape the false voices telling them their only choice is to submit to those who want to exploit them.

Two lies—that of a distant God, too big for us, and that of a trapped human race, too small and sinful to connect with him— combine into one great lie that says God is not near and cannot touch us, and we cannot touch him and enjoy him. Unfortunately, in one way or another our belief systems often are supported by the lie.

There's an old Celtic story about a monk who dies and is interred in the monastery wall. Three days later the other monks are surprised to hear noises coming from the area of the wall in which their brother has been buried. When they remove the stone, to their astonishment they find their brother not only alive but full of excitement and wonderment. He says, "Oh, brothers, I have been there! I've seen it! And it's nothing at all like our theology says it is!" So they put him back in the wall and seal the crypt again.

We can believe God inhabits a different realm, leaving us on our own. We can choose to dismiss God and forge our lesser gods. We can construct our own religion with an absent, even a non-existent God. And when a witness appears, revived to new life by a contrary message of God's closeness, we can shut the witness back up in the crypt of our close-mindedness or we can open our minds and our hearts to the radical idea of a God who makes himself small and enters our world.

Four

The God Who
Makes Himself Small

TWO WOODCUTS OF FRITZ EICHENBERG hang on the wall of my study directly across from where I sit, so I see them every day. One pictures Jesus standing in a breadline seeking food along with homeless people. The other has him sitting at a meal table inside a homeless shelter, and the title is *The Lord's Supper*.

Eichenberg captures the Christian gospel's surprise: God has not only entered our world, he has come in lowliness. He has focused his attention on all the human race, and particularly on those who are most ignored—the marginalized, the poor, the mistreated, the "inferiors," the human leftovers that do not fit in secure social structures. So much for a God too great or too far! laughs the gospel. Something strange is taking place here, a paradox of divinity, a God acting un-Godlike to help us grasp who he *really* is. He is a lover going out of his way and traveling a long way to find his beloved. To borrow an apt line from poet Robert Browning, "Such ever was love's way—to rise, it stoops."

The Incarnation of God

The Incarnation of God is a scandalous thought for those who hold to a platonic view of God as far away and too perfect to get mixed up in the messy terrain of our human life. The gospel goes overboard in telling the story of how messy and lowly and shocking it really is. Jesus is born a temporarily homeless child in a smelly stable in a cow town called Bethlehem, to a humble carpenter and his teenage wife who became pregnant before the wedding. The family flees to Egypt to escape a pogrom of infants being carried out by a king who was told by foreigners that a rival to his throne had just been born. Growing up in Nazareth in the region of Galilee, Jesus works as a lowly carpenter until the age of thirty, when he suddenly sets out to announce the arrival of a very new and different kingdom he names the kingdom of God. He calls twelve ordinary men to be trained as his disciples and future leaders of his movement, and he brings his message to people of modest means and to the poor, the sick and handicapped, and the outcast. He seems largely to ignore the upper classes who have to crash his parties, or seek him out, or intentionally invite him over in order to have time with him. He and his cohort of twelve travel Palestine for three years, a band of homeless men calling people to this very different kind of world he claims to be ushering in. His life ends violently— he is arrested as a threat to both established religion and government stability, and he is executed on a cross between two thieves.

What was God thinking? What was he doing? Where was he going with this? The Apostle Paul summarizes this baffling story in verses that border on the lyrical. Here they are:

> Though he was in the form of God,
>> [Jesus] did not consider being equal with God something to exploit.
> But he emptied himself
>> by taking the form of a slave

and by becoming like human beings.
When he found himself in the form of a human,
    he humbled himself by becoming obedient to the point of
      death,
    even death on a cross. (Philippians 2:6-8)

The gospel story begins with God becoming small and diminished in a world of exalted things, a nobody in a society of somebodies. This is exactly what the Greek word means: Christ made himself nothing, or to translate it even more literally, he emptied himself of his dignity and status, if you like, and became obedient to the mission for which he came and for which he would ultimately give his life.

The Incarnation, God's entry into our world in the flesh and blood of the man Jesus, sets the stage for an overthrow of the stereotype of a totally removed God. Such a God, devoid of distance, is not some new or made-over God. He is the God who has *always* been deeply affected by our lives and has always suffered for our sins. Again and again the Old Testament gives witness to his anger and hurt over how those he loves ignore, betray, and humiliate him. Some of the prophets, and especially Hosea, portray him as a lover who longingly searches for the beloved who has spurned him. The New Testament does not introduce us to a now-different God who decides to suffer over his lost family. It invites us to see God for who he really is and has been all along. The difference is that his heartbreak now becomes the broken heart of Jesus. His suffering over the centuries becomes the burden of one man hanging on a cross. His enduring love for us is forever exposed in raw action. In Jesus everything is now out in the open for those who are willing to risk seeing such a God.

Here a Greek-based theology, with a Greek-style God, is being assaulted by what the Incarnation throws at it. The Incarnation of God is a frontal attack on our persistent attempts to impersonalize, oversize, and distance God. It undermines the comfort of a God-too-far whom we can either refashion or dismiss for our convenience, and it creates the disturbance of a God-too-close, whose love sees us as humans created in his image and calls us to the terrifying prospect of being nothing less than who we are.

God invites us to find our way to him in the flesh and blood of Jesus, a man who walked among us and is still doing so in the Spirit. He invites us to meet him in the small, common, ordinary ways he chooses to reveal himself. He touches our lives by his closeness, and there we find his true greatness. This is the miracle we celebrate in the Christmas story. In the vibrant, vulnerable closeness of the small Child, we meet God.

Keitha and I bought a humble nativity arrangement to display during our first Christmas season together as husband and wife. Over time the paint on the figures has faded and the stable has become so worn as to appear realistic (unlike some of the prettier nativities we now have). Despite the shabby appearance we still display it at Christmas, and could not imagine neglecting to do so. Each year as we bring up the Christmas decorations from the basement, we look for it first. My fondest memory of this nativity is of our two little daughters putting the scene together, each one alternating the placement of the figures, with the youngest always having the privilege of lastly placing the baby Jesus in the manger. I can still hear her exclaim as she did so, "Jesus is born!" as if it were happening right then. I believe it was.

The Presence of God

Our daughter's childhood words inhabit my thoughts and feelings with a reality that, in one way or another, dawns on my life every day: The Incarnation has not gone away. Jesus is born again and again; he is here to stay. He is the embodiment of a promise Jewish theologian Martin Buber concluded is the very meaning of the name of God revealed to Moses when God called

the runaway to return to Egypt and lead his people to a Promised
Land. When anyone asks who sent you, says God to Moses, tell
them I-will-be-there (Yahweh) has sent you (Exodus 3:14). Tell
them I am the always-there-for-you God. Hundreds of years later,
it all becomes materially real in the person of Jesus, whose presence literally means Immanuel ("God is with us"). Yes, Jesus *is*
born every day. Yes, Jesus blesses his followers with the promise
of his presence, just as he did his first disciples in the words of his
farewell: "Look, I myself will be with you every day until the end
of this present age" (Matthew 28:20b).

Where do we see him? Not where fanfares are blaring or
awards are given out. We see him in the small ways: A baby is
born and we see the blessing of hope, a life is saved and we see
the precious worth of another human, a calling of God is obeyed
and we see the creative power of a life lived for others. When do
we sense his presence? Not when we are celebrating our personal
success, or our religion's advancement, or the prosperity of our
version of the gospel. We sense his presence when, in the humble
places of our day, we see him fashioning an extraordinary soul in
an ordinary person, or making a miracle to upset the merely mun-
dane, or revealing himself in the exquisite delight of a child. Jesus
let the secret out in person: God is everywhere, and he invades
the consciousness of those who look for him in the small places of
their lives and live in the expectation of the unanticipated.

God comes to those who are looking for the blessing of his
presence more than the benefits of his presents. In Psalms 17 and
27, David's desire is to gaze upon "the Lord's beauty" (Psalm 27:4)
and to "be filled full by seeing [the Lord's] image" (Psalm 17:15).
He asks God to save him from those "whose only possession is
their fleeting life" (17:14), those seduced by the ephemeral, those
who live in the shallows of favors from lesser gods and who avoid
the possibility of God's real presence, which may come in quiet
but passionate simplicity, like a lover's tryst, a moment long remembered. When Jesus came to earth, with nothing earthly to

offer, he gave us the only thing he had to give: himself—every throb of his compassionate heart and every ounce of his surrendered body, his poured-out presence. And he told his little band of disciples a few days before the death he knew was coming that his presence would always be with them. Over the centuries following his death, many in the church would pursue the power more than the presence; but the true followers of the incarnate Christ would continue to find him where he lowered himself and made himself known in humility. From this place, and this place alone, he calls us to follow him. In fact, he calls us to *be* him.

Our Presence with Others

It is astounding how many of those who hold a membership in a Christian church do not get it. They may understand the Incarnation of God is the miraculous foundation on which the Christian message must rest, but they do not understand, or want to understand, the Incarnation points the way for followers of Jesus actually to *live* their lives. For them, Christians are people who gratefully reap the benefits of God moving in with us in the person of Jesus to rescue us from our sins and their consequences. They do not, however, see themselves as unavoidably called by Jesus to live the radically incarnational life he lived.

Let me explain what I mean by that. The Incarnation of Christ is far more than the event Christians celebrate at Christmas. The birth of Jesus was only the beginning of the Incarnation. The Incarnation was Jesus' way of life from his birth to his death. Jesus was not God playing human; he was God *being* human. The writer of the Letter to the Hebrews in the New Testament emphasizes this claim by using phrases such as, "he too shared in their humanity.... He had to be made like his brothers and sisters in every way" (2:14, 17), and he was "tempted in every way that we are" (4:15). The Jesus I meet in the New Testament is not some phantom pretending or parading as a human. For good reason, the early church came to the conclusion that those in the church who diminished the authentic humanness of Jesus were contradicting the very heart of the Christian gospel. The evangelist John announces the good news that in Jesus "the Word became flesh and made his home among us" (John 1:14). In his first letter he says that "every spirit that confesses that Jesus Christ has come as a human is from God" (I John 4:2). The Incarnation, the becoming-human of God, was not negotiable. The humanness of Jesus, the way he lived among us, the way he was present with people and cared about the small things of their lives, the way he loved them, beginning with the least of them—all this was of utmost significance, not least because Jesus calls us to live in the same way.

How do we manage to miss the point? Obviously, it has something to do with the way we are living, confined to our comfort zones. It is fed by our tendency to forget Christian faith is a way of life, and then to reduce it to doctrines. Doctrines are important. God gives us brains, and we should use them to think through, understand, and express our faith in words and concepts that have meaning for us. This is what we call theology. We must not forget, however, the gospel is a story, the story of God's life with us. It invites us to enter the story and be a part of that life; and, in particular, it invites us to allow the story of Jesus to become our story and to allow it to change us and to change the way we live. Christians differ on some points of doctrine or interpret them in different ways. What is clear truth for us all is that Jesus calls us to a way of life that mirrors his own.

If mirroring the life of Jesus means anything, it means being fully present with others. The God in whose image we are created chooses to be present with us. Jesus is rightly called the man for others. This engagement with other persons, this willingness to be present with them in love, with whatever attentiveness and self-emptying this involves, is largely what it means to be human, to live in the image of God.

I am convinced there is a relationship between our struggle to connect with God and our struggle to connect with each other. Our making of God an idea rather than a person depersonalizes *all* our relationships. When we see God as a perfect ideal by which we are measured rather than an active participant with whom we live and interact, we have distanced him from us, and us from each other. If my life is centered in measuring up to God's high expectations, I will ignore those around me as I strive—and inevitably fail—to meet the impossible standard.

God calls us to become ourselves with others. If there is any measuring up worth pursuing, it is the measuring up to our calling to share compassion with all, and especially those who have received very little compassion in their lives.

It begins with those we are closest to: "Love each other just as I have loved you," says Jesus (John 15:12). Sometimes a person shows little concern for those in his immediate circle. One might think it is easiest to love those closest to us, especially our family. Experience teaches us, however, we can take the gift of our loved ones for granted as we immerse ourselves in other pursuits.

I well remember the elderly gentleman in one of the churches my wife and I pastored who broke down and cried in a private moment I had with him. He was a retired pastor himself, and his tears revealed his profound sorrow and regret that he had been present with his sons very little when they were growing up, because he had carried out what he considered his sacred duty at the time: to throw himself fully into his important work. To that day, his sons resented having been taken for granted. Who of us who have very demanding occupations have not at certain times suddenly become aware we have been working ourselves to an excess that threatens to rob us of the gift of being present with our loved ones? I certainly have. If we are honest with ourselves, honest enough to see when we have not been present with those closest to us, and humble enough to confess our negligence, we can begin to release our love through a patient attentiveness. We can affirm their value as persons and their importance to our own lives.

I am not suggesting a total immersion in the lives of our families. It is possible to be so present with those closest to us that we are, ironically, *not* truly present. When persons cannot let go of one another, when they are tied together by fear of letting themselves each be individuals and threatened by the possibility of one another's absence, being truly present is not possible. We cannot be present unless we are willing to be ourselves with each other and give each other freedom. Perhaps the most crucial choice that must be made in a close relationship is whether to cling to and smother all the time or, along with times of closeness, risk letting go. Real intimacy happens in the counterpoint of closeness and separateness.

The gospel story has a moment of profound insight about this when John's Gospel records Jesus' intimate moments with his disciples leading up to his arrest and crucifixion. Jesus is very aware of what is coming. He is setting the stage for it with his closest disciples, preparing them for their lives following his death and for their future leadership in his movement. The disciples are profoundly grieved over the news Jesus will soon leave them for good. His surprising response to their grief is to share the *benefits* of his absence. He says, "I assure you that it is better for you that I go away" (John 16:7). In his absence he can be present with them in a new way. He will send his Spirit, whom he calls "the Companion," who will "guide [them] in all truth." (John 16:5-15). Along with the pain of separation, they will discover the freedom of his trust in them. His presence with them, and theirs with him, will be different and all the richer. One of the things that makes this story so transformative is this affirmation of absence as crucial to genuine presence. We can be present with others, including those closest to us, only if we can discover the gift of intimacy in their absence, as the disciples finally were able to do after Jesus' departure in the flesh.

The gospel, of course, does not stop with Jesus now being present with his disciples in a new and different way nor with his disciples discovering how to be present with one another. There is something far bigger underway. Jesus calls his disciples to be present with the entire world of people. The call begins with the announcement in John's Gospel that the coming of Jesus is the embodiment of God's love for the entire world (John 3:16). It becomes marching orders for all his followers when he is resurrected and commissions them to "go and make disciples of all nations." (Matthew 28:19).

"All nations" does not say Christianity will become a dominant world religion. Rather, it is the good news that in Jesus the welcoming kingdom of God is here, the door is open, and *everyone* is invited. The message has no legitimacy where the important people are seen to be those at the top of the social order, however that social order is defined—national identity, financial assets, political power, stardom, church position, to give some examples. It has legitimacy only where we take the radical step of recognizing that real importance can be discovered only when we free ourselves from the idolatry of national or social position and enter the level playing field of human worth. This affirms the small people but also the prominent ones who no longer need to hide behind their power and influence to feel they are important.

The willingness to be small opens the door to God's presence. We see it in the woodcuts of Eichenberg where Jesus stands in the breadline and shares the humble meal at a homeless shelter. We see it in the early Celtic priests, who lived simply among the common people, showing them the glory of God in the world around them and the joy of God in the small things. We see it in Francis of Assisi, for whom miracles were big things in small wrappings, and in Mother Theresa, who found the face of Christ in the suffering poor of Calcutta. We see it in Brother Lawrence, the seventeenth-century monk who met Christ daily while performing the humblest of tasks. We see it in humble people everywhere who live *incarnationally* and find God *present* in the world they can touch, *near* in the people they can reach.

You and I can find him in these same ways. He is the God of small things—the people, places, moments, and matters we encounter on our journey. He is the God who wants to save us from our self-diminishing obsessions. He wants to give us each other. He wants to give us himself.

part 3

How God Saves Us *from* Our Obsession with Greatness

Five

The God of
Small Things

MARGARET MOORE IS ONE of my personal heroes and certainly a hero of the faith. For many years she served as a Salvation Army missionary in Rhodesia, before it became Zimbabwe. At that time the country was in a very dangerous state. The repressive racist government was under attack by guerilla insurgents. Sometimes teenage boys disappeared in the night from the school where she taught, either because they wanted to join the rebels or because the secret police had arrested them as rebel sympathizers and supporters. The boys were often never heard from again.

Moore wrote that one day she sat on a low thick branch and stared, unseeing, at Arum lilies,

> . . . living in that dark abyss
> Where one tries to hide from one's own betrayals.

She went on to say,

Nothing spoke to me:
Not the strong wood,
Not the familiar line of limb framing sky and cloud,
Not anything in my past,
Not anyone in my present,
And certainly not God.
                    (1969, 536)

And then it happened. A three-year-old African child came out of nowhere and crawled on to her lap and fell asleep. Moore did not know if the child was lost or was escaping parental wrath. She cradled him, covering him with her jacket when the sun began to sink and the air became chilly. "And there I sat," said Moore, "warmed back into humanity by a child's animal trust of arms and lap." God's light into her darkness, an Incarnation bringing her back from her loneliness and pain (1969, 536).

The beauty and power of what happened that day lay in the utter simplicity and smallness of the experience. In a part of the world where poverty is rampant and racism grounds a social order brutally enforced, an African child finds his way to a white lady who is searching in vain for a healing peace. Margaret Moore is disquieted by the knowledge that although she is contributing to the lives of the young people she is teaching and tutoring, she is able to do so only by a tacit compromise with a repressive racist government. She is also trying to make some sense of it, trying to envision a future for this land and these people she loves. The consolation she is looking for comes as a tiny ray of light entering her world in the form of a child, a small matter in the order of things. In this small moment, in this small place, she is drawn back to the God of small things and to the power of God to speak and act in the smallest ways through the smallest person.

Small People

Such is the way of the God of the gospel, it seems. In the Bible we meet a God who loves to work through small people to expose his presence and tell us what is on his heart and what he is doing or is about to do. Consider a teenager named Mary who lives in the small town of Nazareth in Galilee. From all the evidence we have, she is not of high birth; she is, in fact, engaged to a carpenter. An angel appears to Mary and tells her she is highly favored because the Lord is with her. She is so favored she will give birth to the Liberator-Messiah of Israel. The news floors her, not only because Israel has been waiting for this liberation for a long, long time but also because it is beyond her comprehension that God would choose someone of such humble state as she to bear the Messiah. When she sees her cousin Elizabeth, she can hardly contain herself. She breaks out into ecstatic song.

Over the years the song found its way into Luke's Gospel (Luke 1:46-55). It is commonly know as the *Magnificat*. What makes Mary's song so revealing is, first, that it celebrates the miracle of God taking a servant and blessing her with this astounding privilege. Even more revealing is another surprise in the song: the prophecy of how this Messiah will turn everything upside down. The message rings with such certainty it is spoken as if the prophecy is already in the process of being fulfilled. Mary sings,

> [God] has pulled the powerful
>> down from their thrones
>> and lifted up the lowly.
> He has filled the hungry with good things
>> and sent the rich away empty-handed.
>
> Luke 1:52-53

When it comes to people, the gospel is an inversion of the social systems invented and practiced by a fallen human race. In one form or another, all civilizations and societies have rulers on thrones (whether we call them kings and queens, dictators, premiers, prime ministers, governors, or presidents). And they also have the rich (whether the wealth is honestly earned, inherited, received through government favor, or obtained through crime, violent or white-collar). Mary's song says the rulers will be brought down and the rich sent away empty-handed. Obviously, this does not always happen, at least not in this life on earth. So how do we make sense of the prophecy? What does it mean for us?

If we are among the majority in the Western world, the prophecy has particular meaning. In comparison to the rest of the world, we are highly privileged materially. For us, the prophecy says our power and prominence in no way enhance our value as persons. To reject the prophecy is to continue to live under the illusion that these things actually give our lives some kind of air-tight authenticity. Choosing the way of Jesus does not necessarily mean doing what Jesus advised the rich young ruler to do: divest himself of it all and follow him. Like Francis of Assissi, some do. What it does mean in every case is the realization that, stripped of position, prominence, and wealth (or even the dream of having them), we can see ourselves for who we really are: the humble, the hungry.

Those of us who know ourselves in this stripped-down state are ready to enter the upside-down kingdom of Jesus. Further, we will see our power and our wealth very differently, as something to hold lightly and to use wisely and compassionately, for the benefit of others. We will confess that, apart from the power and wealth, we may be empty of spirit and meager of character. This awareness is a gift because it opens us to the only path of liberation: humility. Humility is starting where we really are and finding the gift of God there, and not in the somewhere else of our ambition to be bigger and better than others. Our hubris can be healed only when we allow ourselves to become small. God works through small people like Mary, whatever place they may inhabit in the social order.

Mary's song is a poor girl's song about a God who impoverishes himself in Jesus, who spends most of his time among the poor of the land. He announces a strange Kingdom that has no place of honor based on wealth or political power. Instead, he offers his compassion, and he invites his listeners to love one another. Love is the great equalizer. One cannot love from a higher position. Love requires personal abandonment, a divestiture of the social, economic, political, or hierarchical artifices we think make us somebody of worth. Only love does that, and the loving requires the divestiture, the humility. It descends, never condescends. This is what God is teaching us in Jesus.

Is it possible for someone of high position or considerable wealth to be on a level playing field with someone occupying a much "lower" position in the social order? Of course it is. It requires, however, an exceptional humility, almost a rebellion against appropriate class behavior and an offence against the self-protective firewall of social distinction. Where does this humility come from? How is it possible, to use Jesus' analogy, for a camel to go through the eye of a needle, for a rich or famous person to enter the kingdom of God? It is a grace given to love persons rather than things, to set one's heart on the small, intimate setting of a relationship, unencumbered by the divisive barrier of position and wealth. It is owning the self-emptying example of the God who emptied himself and became one of us—specifically, one of the lowest of us—and embracing this example as the model of our own self-emptying liberation. It is the grace we receive that enables us to recognize we can only discover our true humanity by knowing ourselves stripped of the pretenses we can acquire through position and wealth. It is the grace God gives us to become small.

The smallest book in the Bible is a letter of only twenty-five verses tucked away in the New Testament between Titus and Hebrews. It is a letter from the Apostle Paul to Philemon, a Christian believer living in Colosse in Asia Minor. Philemon, a person of some means, was a slave owner. Slave ownership was common among those of wealth. Onesimus, his slave, had run away, or at least had failed to return from an assignment for fear of punishment for some wrong he had done and suspected had been discovered. The runaway had found his way to Paul and sought his help. It is likely he had also been led to faith through Paul's ministry. At some point in all this, Paul was arrested for his "dangerous" teaching and proselytizing. When he sensed that the time had come to send Onesimus back to be reconciled to his owner, his intervention had to be limited to a letter from jail.

The issue was most sensitive, as slave owners had the right to punish a runaway slave with death. Philemon, however, was a Christian, and Onesimus had now come to faith. This meant that the relationship between them had been radically changed. In the social order of the day, that relationship was still defined by Philemon's ownership of Onesimus. In the kingdom of God, however, in the new order of God's family, they were now brothers in Christ. This new reality meant Philemon could no longer treat Onesimus as a lesser person. It meant that forgiveness was called for, not as an act of condescension on Philemon's part, but as the natural expression of family love and solidarity.

At this point in his ministry, Paul was held in high regard by many converts within the still-young Christian movement. He was certainly esteemed by Philemon, and perhaps Paul had been a spiritual mentor to him. In the letter, however, he does not approach Philemon on the basis of Paul's higher position in the church. He does not use the leverage of his rightful spiritual authority. He appeals to him as a "brother" and a "partner." He then brings Onesimus into the same family circle. Receive Onesimus back, writes Paul, as "no longer a slave [but] as a dearly loved brother" (Philemon 16).

We do not know the outcome of the story. Onesimus himself was the bearer of the letter. Hopefully, Philemon received Onesimus back as a brother and forgave him. He may have administered some appropriate discipline, which is part of all true acts of forgiveness. The discipline may have also included Philemon pledging to treat Onesimus in a kinder manner. Onesimus may well have remained a slave of Philemon. The social order and economy of that day were built on slavery, and some slave owners treated their slaves fairly. Yet Paul was inviting Philemon to go beyond even the fairness of a good master. He was inviting him to see Onesimus outside the barriers of the social system and to treat him as a brother. He was inviting him to risk stepping outside the power of his social status and becoming small.

There is a hunger in all of us for community and relationships. There is, however, a huge barrier to it, and that is the fear of our insignificance. Because of the fear we feel worthless unless we are in a better, stronger, or more advantageous or prestigious position than someone else. We see our worth residing not in ourselves, as persons created in the image of God himself, but in the acquired social symbols of accomplishment, success, and status.

Yet, on a deeper level, we seem to know better. Our literature, movies, and TV series are replete with stories of social barriers being breached for friendship, romance, or compassion, and often a huge price is paid for it. We find such stories of transcending behavior powerful and appealing, just as we find the depiction of the cruel exclusions of social, economic, racial, and ethnic discrimination so repulsive. Perhaps we experience in these stories a kind of cleansing catharsis for our consciences in order to relieve the guilt of our own compromises. It is easier to condemn behavior read in a book or seen on a screen than to admit that we are guilty of such behavior as well. Becoming small by refusing to abide by the borders that separate and seduce us is a risky business. The borders are so well protected, and defended.

Jesus, the greatest barrier-breaker ever, invites us to take the risk. During his three-year ministry, he managed to offend the pride of just about every social class save the poor and the foreigners. He gravitated to the small people who lived outside the borders that defined and protected privilege. He shamelessly spoke one-on-one with Gentiles, those who were not God's "chosen people." He respected women and refused to look down on them. He stood in the breach between a woman taken in adultery and her smug accusers who were about to stone her to death, and he dissolved their claim to a superior righteousness by his simple challenge: "Whoever hasn't sinned should throw the first stone" (John 8:7). He preached in the open air to multitudes of despised commoners. He went to the parties of publicans and sinners. He invited a compromised Jew like Matthew to join him. He said God was more interested in the prayer of a sinner who confessed his sin than in a Pharisee, a spiritual leader who was prepared to defend his own righteousness before God. He went even further when he addressed the chief priests and elders in the Jerusalem temple: "I assure you that tax collectors and prostitutes are entering God's kingdom ahead of you." (Matthew 21:31b). And to top it all off, at the end of Jesus' life as he was dying on a cross, Jesus promised eternity with him in paradise to a thief hanging for his crimes on a cross next to him. With the walls of exclusivity so dangerously weakened, there was no telling what Jesus was letting loose in the world, and where it would lead.

The Christian wave that swept across the Mediterranean world in the centuries after Christ was primarily a movement of small people. To be sure, it had its brilliant apologists and theologians to articulate and defend the faith, as well as some converts of means who helped to support the mission. The records show, however, that most of those who first signed up to follow the obscure Messiah from Nazareth were from the lower classes, including many women, whose status in that world was second-class. One of the common criticisms of the new faith was that its disciples consisted mostly of women and slaves. This observation was meant in disparagement, but it was the ultimate compliment to the movement for its faithfulness to the gospel of a small-becoming God.

As the Christian movement grew, despite repeated attempts to delegitimize the scandalous new religion and execute its most passionate adherents, those who held power and wealth began to join. For many it was a genuine conversion to a God of love and forgiveness embodied in Jesus. The motivation of others was a mixed bag. And still, for others it was a blatantly self-serving decision based on their awareness that the Christian movement was becoming Christianity, the official religion of the Roman Empire, and the only way to legitimize their own power and prosperity. The securing of their privileged place and the possibility of future success necessitated, for some, their conversion. Even as early as the latter half of the first century, opportunists dabbled in a form of the Christian faith, hoping to turn it to their advantage. In his first letter to Timothy, the Apostle Paul alerted his protégé to an emerging prosperity gospel motivating those "who think that godliness is a way to make money" (I Timothy 6:5). It had not taken long for the duplicitous to counterfeit the faith.

Thus began an erosion of the gospel. The small-becoming God became the God who legitimized a social order that had little resemblance to the social order envisioned by Jesus when he described the Kingdom of God. To be sure, the story of Jesus' humility continued to be told, but not as a model all his followers were expected to be able to follow—save for a few extraordinary Christians who were designated "saints." These exemplary Christians were seen as rare iconic figures who were so like Jesus, the overabundant goodness could be extracted and appropriated to the less faithful through penance and prayer. Ironically, identification with the Christian church became for many the respectable cover for a life of shameless self-promotion and even exploitation. It shared scant resemblance to the life of the one they called Lord, and it forgot Jesus the rabbi whose life they, his disciples, were supposed to emulate.

From time to time over the past almost two thousand years, men and women have appeared on the scene as reminders of the life of Jesus. Their lives are messages of hope for us all. They are among us as icons of God-in-the-ordinary, not as iconic celebrities whose goodness is out of reach for the rest of us. Their compassion is their hallmark, their humility their freedom. They are like Dietrich Bonhoeffer, who divested himself of privilege, personal security, and cowering accommodation to a monstrous status quo to oppose Hitler's persecution of Jews at the cost of his own life. Relinquishing all markers of position, status, and security, Bonhoefffer chose instead to surrender his identity to God: "Whoever I am," he wrote, "Thou knowest, O God, I am thine!" (1953, 173). In this humility of a disciple, this powerful smallness, he became free, free enough to walk to a martyr's death.

Bonhoeffer and others like him remind us of the life to which Christ is calling us. They point us to the God of small things. And as we allow ourselves to take them seriously, we hear a call to take ourselves seriously. We hear a call to abandon our pursuit of more, which is not worth the seriousness we ascribe to it. And we hear a call to less, which is worth far, far more than we can see and the social order can value. Those who become small are the ones who really have something to teach us.

Small Places

Small places are woven into the texture of our lives. Mark Twain saw his home in Hartford, Connecticut, as a place of blessing: "Our house was not unsentient matter—it had a heart, and a soul, and eyes to see with; . . . it was of us, and we were in its confidence, and lived in its grace, and in the peace of its benediction" (Van Wyck, 1922). Small places in our lives carry memories that shape us, blessings that honor us, hurts that may still pain us. All of this is woven into the texture of these important small places.

As I advance in years, I find myself drawn more and more to

the small places of my journey. I like to return to the places where I once lived. I remember returning to the home where my family had lived during some of my childhood years in Tampa, Florida. As I stood in front of the house on Branch Avenue, memories emerged with fresh and powerful vividness. I mustered the nerve to ask the single mother who had raised her children there if I could come in and see the rooms where I had spent some important years of my childhood. To my surprise she agreed. Walking through those rooms felt like a retraced pilgrimage, a remembering that drew me closer to my formation as part of a close-knit family. I then walked through the neighborhood, recalling where my friends had lived, the secret places where we had conspired mischief and madness, the open spaces where we had displayed our prowess at touch football or corkball, the huge banyan tree on which we had risked life and limb jumping from branch to branch, the elementary and junior high schools where so many teachers had nurtured my thirst for knowledge.

Some of the other small places of my past that I have visited as an adult now bear little resemblance to the place I remember. Unrelenting change sometimes rearranges our landscapes so radically; when we return there is little to recognize. The church building in downtown Tampa where my parents pastored is no more, the casualty of interstate highway construction. When I went back to where it once stood and saw nothing but concrete, I felt robbed of an important small place. I quietly grieved. I remembered the promise from Matthew's Gospel given to the Apostle Peter, which was always printed on the front of each order of worship bulletin in those days: "And upon this rock I will build my church; and the gates of hell shall not prevail against it" (16:18 KJV). The verse said nothing about concrete! I am left with only my memories about that place, but fortunately those memories are strong, and I cannot be robbed of what that place means to me, and the role it played in who I became.

I fear people who are living in a fast-paced world will lose the small places that hold the tangible memories and give textured meaning to their journey. The triumph of the Internet may be undermining our sense of specific places, making us too available anywhere and keeping us less aware of where we are. Pastor, professor, and speaker Ken Callahan speaks of the importance of roots, place, and belonging in our lives. A rootless person without family who nurtured him, without a group who contributed toward the formation of the person's identity, without connection to places that are sacred, is a soul adrift. In this world of high mobility and instant access, we are in danger of navigating in ever-enlarging landscapes and living nowhere in particular. We are trading our sense of place for places in general, the memories of important small places for places we are only passing through and not seeing.

There are no large places that can fit into our stories, only small places. Our memories cannot contain and treasure the overwhelming details and complexities of expansive locations. Large places are, in fact, fictions we create by merging many small places into one for purposes of governance, order, and commerce. Large cities do not really have character; only the communities that comprise them do. What is the metroplex of London, England? Only an abstraction. The reality is that over the centuries a host of small communities and towns grew together and connected their roads. To this day those roads curve frequently in every direction and successfully confuse every uninitiated driver. (If you haven't been lost in London, you haven't driven there!) The character of London is the widely diverse character of many smaller communities and places, which are the endlessly variegated threads of a complex fabric that as a whole is beyond our grasp. A person loves London because of the specific places within it that have meaning or appeal.

I live in a city that is an infant in age compared to London. Atlanta has grown at a very fast pace over recent decades, and city planners have tried to anticipate the growth with commuter roads and interstate highways. Atlanta is easier to get around in than London. Even in its comparatively short life and even with an expansionist mindset that sometimes undermines the localized flavors of communities absorbed by the grid, Atlanta is still comprised of small communities, each with its unique character and culture. The love I have for Atlanta really has to do with specific neighborhoods where I have lived and special places I visit—small places like Adair Park, Virginia-Highlands, Stone Mountain, Tucker, and even smaller places, including the homes I've lived in, the immediate neighborhoods around them, the schools I have attended, the places where I worked. Large places are places on a map and convenient concepts in our minds. Small places reside in our memories and are treasured in our hearts.

The Bible names many small places as sacred sites. One of the most significant is Bethel, and there is a story behind it (Genesis 28:10-22). Jacob is on the run from Esau, the older brother from whom he had stolen their father Isaac's blessing and promise. Sleeping alone under the desert sky with only a stone as a pillow, Jacob has a dream of angels (messengers) descending and ascending on a ladder from heaven. Above the ladder he sees the Lord and hears him say, "I am the Lord, the God of your father Abraham and the God of Isaac. I will give you and your descendants the land on which you are lying....Every family of earth will be blessed because of you and your descendants....I will not leave you until I have done everything that I have promised you." When Jacob awakes and remembers the dream, he thinks to himself, "The Lord is definitely in this place, but I didn't know it." A small place of no significance has become the venue of an epiphany and a lasting promise of blessing. To commemorate the visitation and to mark the sacredness of this small space, Jacob takes the stone that held his head in sleep and pours oil over it. The town nearby is evidently called Luz, but Jacob names it *Bethel*, meaning "house of God." From that time, Bethel becomes a place of spiritual significance where, over the centuries, many important leaders in Israel return.

It is the place where God speaks. It is even a place God identifies with, for years later he appears again to Jacob, identifying himself as "The God of Bethel" (Genesis 31:15a).

The story of Jesus honors small places. He was born in a small town, Bethlehem, and raised in another small town, Nazareth. He visited people in their homes and traveled to small communities. It was in Jerusalem, the largest city in Judea, where his enemies conspired to arrest, try, and condemn him. He was crucified outside its walls, on a hill called *Golgotha*, which means "the place of the skull," now a small place of profound importance to Christians around the world.

Golgotha reminds us that some of the small places that are significant for us are places of pain and suffering. An adult returns to the house where she grew up and weeps uncontrollably: This is the place she suffered unspeakable abuse. Can she find healing, a cleansing of the memories, the freedom to move on toward wholeness? Another adult returns to the school where he was repeatedly bullied. Can he find freedom from the fear and belittlement? I dare say all of us have at least one such small place where the memories are still hurtful. Can we find release from the hurt? Thankfully, God cares about all the small places of our lives, just as he cared deeply about the unbearable suffering of Jesus on a small hill. And just as in that place of pain Jesus found large redemption, so we may find healing by owning the pain and releasing it to God and the healers he sends our way. We must, however, journey back to the place of trauma in order to begin. It is there, only in that small place, that wholeness begins.

Our lives are a journey through small places. God is in the journey, and where we encounter him in one way or another the location becomes sacred. Some of those locations in our lives have a lasting place in our memories. Over time a few of them may have become redolent with the blessing of someone or the presence of something godly. They may be our holy sites, holding a certain spiritual presence and power.

My mother passed away a few short years ago. A part of her modest estate was the home where she lived for twenty-three years following our father's passing. She died in her sleep there. She left the home to her four children to be divided equally. We decided to put the house on the market. First, however, we hired a contractor to paint the inside and do a few other minor improvements to make it more attractive to prospective buyers. The contractor had not been acquainted with our mother. During the course of his work, when we stopped by to see how it was all progressing, he said something interesting. He said, "There is something about this house, a kind of spirit is here." He did not say it in an eerie way; it sounded like a blessing. I believe it was, and when I occasionally drive by the home, now occupied by a different owner, I pull the car over and receive the blessing again.

Small Moments

Our lives are lived in small moments. More often than we recognize, those moments are open windows. When we look back over our lives, we can probably remember small snatches of time when a window opened and we saw something in a totally different way. Or we discovered something important we had not known. Perhaps we saw ourselves differently. Or we allowed someone to interrupt our busyness and pour out the joy or confusion or pain that was in his heart. Perhaps we heard the voice of God, or felt his nudging. These were small moments that became large. I suspect God was in all of them.

If I were honest with myself, I would have to admit I often missed the open window found in small moments. My mind and even my heart were not in the moment; they were somewhere else. That "somewhere else" was not necessarily a bad place; it was a place of distraction. (Let me hasten to say that sometimes such flights of fancy are a blessing. I have found this to be the case when I am in required attendance at some utterly boring event. At such times, the distraction itself has occasionally *been* the open window to something far more profitable to my spirit!) What I regret are the times when the moment before me was a window I failed to open. It may have been someone to whom I was giving only brief, formal attention, and I realized later there was something more on his heart. It may have been an idea from someone about a project we were working on that I politely ignored even while acknowledging it, because it did not fit into my scheme. It may have been a time I was so preoccupied with a problem I was inaccessible even to my family. It may have been a period of pervasive boredom that desensitized me to my surroundings, and I saw no windows to open.

Kathleen Norris has written an insightful book on our struggle with living in the moment. *Acedia and Me* explores Norris' own battle with acedia, a word that identifies both the experience of boredom and the underlying, spirit-killing dimensions of it. The word acedia emerges very early in the history of the Christian Church, first of all in monasteries where the monks sometimes reached a state where they could no longer find meaning or feel passion for the routines and tasks of their ordered lives. They labeled this condition acedia and described it as "the noonday demon." Why did they call it the noonday demon? Because it attacked in broad daylight. This threat to the spirit may be what the psalmist had in mind when he spoke not only of "the sickness that prowls in the dark" but also of "the destruction that ravages at noontime." (Psalm 91:6)

For a long time acedia was considered a malady that monks battled because they were so confined and therefore subject to boredom. Gradually, however, the Church began to realize this demon attacks us all. They came to take it so seriously that it was included as one of the Seven Deadly Sins, all the more deadly because it was hidden in broad daylight and therefore most difficult to detect. Norris tells, and gives proof, that the malady is widespread today, especially when our days are fast-paced and our moments too fleeting to be received, and also when our days slow down but the moments now seem empty. If acedia is a demonic strategy, the demon's purpose is to get us not to care. It may be someone or something else we are not caring about because we are too absorbed with our own plans or fears to give a moment elsewhere. Or it may be ourselves we are not caring about because we are too driven to stop for a moment to let someone else, or God, be honest with us and care about us. Our defeat is that we are either letting the demon shut us down or we are overcompensating with compulsive activity and productivity, trying to convince ourselves or someone else that we do in fact care, when in truth we are too depleted to do so. Compulsive consumerism in our Western world may be one way we mask or attempt to escape acedia. We busy ourselves pursuing the latest merchandise, hoping our obsession will free us from the boredom. And of course we discover it does not.

If we remain in the small moments and allow ourselves to experience them, they become gifts to be received. We can learn to nurture those moments. We can learn to wait for God to touch us any time. Henri Nouwen advises us

> to stay where we are and live the situation out to the full in the belief that something hidden there will manifest itself to us. Impatient people are always expecting the real thing to happen somewhere else and therefore want to go elsewhere. The moment is empty. But patient people dare to stay where they are. Patient living means to live actively in the present and wait there. Waiting, then, is not passive. It involves nurturing the moment, as a mother nurtures the child that is growing in her womb. (2004, 38)

Time is not a quantity to be measured, manipulated, and mastered. It is a moment to wait for, a fullness to be received, and a response to be given.

In his letter to Christians in Ephesus, the Apostle Paul invites his readers to awaken from the sleep of darkness and "live [their] lives as children of light." He urges them, "Don't participate in the unfruitful actions of darkness." He invites them to welcome "every sort of goodness, justice, and truth." "Wake up!" he says, and "take advantage of every opportunity" (Ephesians 5:6-16). He is not counseling them to make their moments more productive for their individual purposes; he is counseling them to be more fruitful with the life God has given them. He is encouraging them to listen for a word from God spoken or unspoken, to look for God's will in their moments, to receive the spirit of God himself in the small moments that can become epiphanies of grace.

Living well is largely a matter of knowing what time it is— that is, if we understand time as a fullness to be received rather than a ticking clock to beat. Life comes to us as opportune moments, not as a blank page. As the wise writer of Ecclesiastes puts it, "There's a season for everything and a time for every matter under the heavens" (Ecclesiastes 3:1). We do not arbitrarily say such things as: "Today I'm deciding to be born, or to die, or to mourn, or to dance, or to speak, or not to speak"—and so on. We do these and other important things because the moment calls for it. We do them because it is time. We do them because we are responding to the moment. This is not to say we are not free. We are free to respond to the moment or not, and we are free to reject what the moment is saying. If we respond to the moment in a positive way, we are free in how we do so. The opportune moments that come our way are not God's attempts to keep us in line; they are his open windows to new realities and his gracious invitations to a new phase of the journey we are taking. They are not special to us alone; they always open doors to others.

The actual value of what we do with the small moments of our lives has nothing to do with how our actions are recognized, honored, praised, or eulogized by others. The beauty of a moment well lived, an opportunity for goodness taken, an act of extraordinary generosity done, are enhanced by their anonymity. Consider, for example, the endless opportunities to share our resources with others. Humble, generous people make small moments truly significant all the more when they keep their generosity and compassion hidden.

Once, however, Jesus is caught peeking. He is in the temple with his disciples while offerings are being given. The rich are making their contributions when along comes a poor widow. She puts in a measly two copper coins—not very impressive. Then, why is Jesus so taken by her offering? He turns to his disciples and says, "I assure you that this widow has put in more than them all. All of them are giving out of their spare change. But she from her hopeless poverty has given everything she had to live on" (Luke 21:1-4). Whether or not Jesus is speaking in hyperbole when he says, "everything she had to live on," is beside the point. The point is that the one who is least in a position to give so much of her meager income is the one who is able to open her heart the widest. This is a small moment of great beauty.

Some moments are life-changing. James E. Loder calls them transforming moments in his book *The Transforming Moment: Understanding Convictional Experiences*. They are unexpected encounters with the kind of truth that makes a claim on us. This is because God is present in them in some way, inviting us to take a leap of faith and be converted. The Bible is replete with accounts of such moments. There is the moment Abram hears a voice telling him to pick up stakes and move his family to a land far to the west (Genesis 12:1); it is a transforming moment because it takes hold of Abram and sets him on a journey to become Abraham (a name change), the father of God's chosen people. A priest named Isaiah has a transforming moment during temple worship (Isaiah 6); it calls him to a crucial prophetic role in the history of Israel. A rabbi named Saul of Tarsus is blinded on a road to Damascus on his way to persecute the new sect of Christ-followers; he hears a voice calling into question this enterprise to which he is so seriously committed. Suddenly he seems to realize he is persecuting the truth; he becomes Paul (another name change) and champions Christian faith throughout the Mediterranean world (Acts 9).

Let us not be over-awed, however, by the momentousness of these specific transforming moments about which we read. They are models for us *all*, stories we can all enter into in some way or another. We are all Abraham: We are called in some way to move beyond our settled life and take the risk of fulfilling our promise and potential. We are all Isaiah: We are called to speak truth in all honesty and with all compassion. We are all Paul: We are called to leave our religion of fear and hatred behind and open our arms to the world. All of us are called to live, as best we can, in openness to the transforming moment when God appears in one way or another and knocks or nudges us toward change. For us, that moment may not come with clash of cymbal or celebrity. It will more likely come like "the still, small voice" Elijah heard. After the powerful wind, earthquake, and fire spoke nothing, the gentle whisper ushered him into God's presence. Elijah's admitted depletion left him open to God's moment, and God gave him the blessing of trust and an open door to the next phase of his calling. And so it is with us: In a small moment God steals up on us like a gentle whisper, blesses us, and trusts us with something beyond us that, strangely, *is* us.

This is our calling: to risk an eager expectancy that does not yet know what is coming our way. We may have been taught to look for our big break, but God seems only interested in a breakthrough. The miracle comes from God, not our wishful thinking, not our ambitious plans. We cannot force the moment, we can only live in the smallness of it, with humility and openness. Then, we just might be surprised, or even shocked, by God.

God's moment may be a slight correction to course or perhaps a complete change of course. It may come when we are riding high and seriously need some humility, feeling worthless and need affirmation, or feeling unsuccessful and need encouragement. It may come when we are in a painful place and need hope or when we are in a secure place and need unsettling. It may come when we are confused and need guidance or when we think we are absolutely right and need to be confused. It may come when we risk looking into someone's face and seeing something on his or her heart, and then coming to a halt and truly listening. It may come in a very small, private moment, hidden for all time to the rest of the world, but a transforming moment for us, like a small child lying on Margaret Moore's lap. It may come in a moment unnoticed by everyone else, like the gift of all she had from an impoverished widow, a small act that challenges us all because Jesus was there and noticed unmatched generosity. All such moments, most of them small by our usual measurements, are God's gift to us. They can connect us, lift us, humble us, even strip us of our addiction to acquisitiveness, and they can change and even transform us.

Small Matters

We have lived through many decades of more and more. Enlargement and expansion have been our watchwords. The mantras of our lives are variations on the same theme: We must have hefty salary increases, make more money, acquire more assets, develop our resources, expand market share. Our business must buy out other businesses. We must get a bigger and better home, or perhaps have a second home, even a third. Gross domestic product must increase at a healthy rate. In our culture, these are normal expectations; in fact, they are seen as our *right*, and when we are able to achieve them in one way or another, all is right with our world.

The market crashes, crushed under the weight of the blind optimism gone bad. The pursuit of more and more (oblivious to the dangerously fragile backing of borrowing-on-borrowing) must sooner or later confront the deception behind such madness. Sometimes the correction is huge, and people suffer either from their own addiction to more and more or from the addictions of others. Lessons learned, however, can be short-lived. The addiction to more and more proves to be a demon waiting for the return to normalcy. Then it can seduce us with its lie that the painful correction was an aberration that is unlikely to return any time soon. And so the race resumes. We cannot seem to help ourselves.

During the correction period, however, the time of less and less, something good may have happened. We may have rediscovered how rich less can be. We may have experienced a healthier moderation in diet, a freedom from compulsive buying, a release from the driven life. More important, we may have spent more time conversing and connecting with family and friends. We may have started listening more to what our heart was teaching us. We may have started learning how less can be more.

When such times are received as gifts rather than harsh sentences, small matters take on a new significance. Little things that did not matter or that we had very little time for when we were caught up in our expansionist rat race suddenly seem to be matters of greater importance. We discover these little things give our lives deeper value. We experience the satisfaction of simple living and close community. We begin to realize we cannot enjoy the simple beauties of life if we are constantly on the move, rarely able to stop, look, listen, and take in the many treasures at our fingertips, nor can we really know love if we love what God never meant for us to love. As Reuel Howe observes in *Man's Need and God's Action*, God made people to be loved and things to be used, and our sin is that we love things and use people (1953, 19–30). Many relationships are destroyed by a fear of intimacy and an escape to the love of work and its material returns. This is true whether the work-addicted person is successful in achieving monetary success and respect in the community or his obsessive work yields little material return or status.

The small matters of our lives offer the alternative to our self-diminishing obsession with more wealth and more status. By our attentiveness to small matters, we honor the God of small things, the God who became small for us in Jesus. It is no accident that Jesus went around talking about small matters. He avoided abstractions and philosophies. He spoke of matters like the planting of seeds, the harvesting of crops, the savor of salt, the bridegroom's joy, loving one another—all specific and down-to-earth. He found in such smallness ways to understand the kingdom of God. He spoke disparagingly of both wealthy people who stored up more and more of their assets (Luke 12:16-21) and rulers who enjoyed exercising power over others (Mark 10:42-45). When the rich young ruler came to Jesus to ask what he still lacked to inherit eternity (i.e., enter the kingdom of God), Jesus saw he was very devout in following the Torah (the essential Jewish law), but his personal identity was tied to his wealth. Jesus' shocking stipulation to this basically good man was far beyond what could reasonably be expected from him. What right did Jesus have to push him to divest himself of his resources? My guess is it was the right to invite the man to do what Jesus invites us all to do: to walk away from what is destroying our soul. Jesus believed what this particular rich man needed to do was to shrink his life in order to allow his soul to expand, to breathe again and be nurtured back to life, to find where the worthwhile things really lie.

And where is that? Where do we find value that lasts? Many people seem to be of the opinion the value of the life we live resides in the dimensions of our achievement. They think they will be remembered for their accomplishments. When they come to the end of their lives, they want people to honor them for how they stood out from their peers, what was unique about their contribution. This may well give a certain level of satisfaction. I am of the opinion, however, there is something that gives far more value to our lives than this, a value that is never lost. It has to do with small matters like sharing intimate moments with someone you love, sharing compassion with someone God brings to your doorstep, sharing hope with someone in despair. It has to do with our attentiveness to the little things around us that are gifts of God. It is knowing by our own experience that miracles surround us, that the kingdom of God can make a surprise appearance in our everyday world or in a chance encounter. This is how God links with us and we with him. These are incarnational moments when our vision is not directed to the heights but down to ground level, to the small matters in which God is drawing near. When we come to the end of our lives, our attention to such small matters is what will bring us deep joy and satisfaction because we have met each other in those places, and we have met God, and nothing, not death itself, can rob us of those encounters.

It was said of Ignatius of Loyola that he had a genius for seeing the spiritual significance of small matters. One of his students wrote this about him:

> We often saw how even the smallest things could make his spirit soar upwards to God, who even in the smallest things is the Greatest. At the sight of a little plant, a leaf, a flower or a fruit, an insignificant worm or a tiny animal, Ignatius could soar free above the heaven and reach through into things which lie beyond the senses. (2004, 197)

Perhaps what the mystics best teach us is how we touch heaven in small matters and ways. When we find blessing in the small people, places, moments, and matters of our lives, the small-becoming God is there. If we allow ourselves to become small, we can see him.

If we humble ourselves, we can even know him. John the Baptist is seen by Christians as the forerunner to Jesus, preparing the way for the true Messiah. John, however, had quite a following of his own. Large crowds were attending his rallies and taking his message of repentance seriously. When Jesus appeared on the scene, John had to make a decision: compete with Jesus for his own share of the market of potential followers, or humble himself. He was asked again and again if he, John, were the Messiah they were anxiously awaiting. His answer was that he was only a voice crying in the wilderness, announcing that the Messiah would soon appear and urging his listeners to get ready by repenting of their sins. He released his own disciples to Jesus (John 1:35-37), and he explained to his followers that the impact of Jesus must increase and his own impact decrease (3:30).

It is interesting that John still did not seem fully to understand what kind of Messiah Jesus was. He expected big things to come about, and quickly. When this did not happen, he began to have doubts about Jesus. After John was imprisoned for his own prophetic criticism of people in high places, wondering whether Jesus would really usher in the kingdom of God, he sent messengers to Jesus to ask if he really were the expected Messiah. The answer Jesus sent back to John was a shocking inversion of the messianic message that had been sweeping the land for years. With no accompanying claim actually to be the Messiah, Jesus' answer was simply this: "Go and tell John what you hear and see: the blind receive sight, the lame walk, the lepers are cleansed, the deaf hear, the dead are raised, and the poor have good news brought to them. And blessed is anyone who takes no offense at me" (Matthew 11:4-6 NRSV). Jesus aimed for the small people, visited the small places, made small moments important, and elevated small matters. He was telling us, "If you want to see me and know me, humble yourself. Become small. Only then will I not be offensive to you. Only then will you understand who I am and what I am about."

Jesus invites us all to the freedom in which he himself lived on earth. He beckons us to humble ourselves down to our true size by giving up our obsession with greatness created by our fear of insignificance. There *is* no insignificance in who or what our loving God has created, only in the illusions and deceptions we have let ourselves believe. Our lives are never too small for God to care about because his love has infinitely long arms. We are never too far away for him to touch us because he is already there. The question is not whether or not God is great. The question is whether or not he is good and gracious, showing up like a still, small voice, a little child, a poor widow, a quiet blessing, a kind gesture, a loving word where we are and when we least expect.

Six

The God of Extraordinary
Goodness and Grace

THE SETTING IS APPOMATTOX in April 1865. The American Civil War is almost over. The country has paid an exorbitant price to end the evil of slavery. Two great generals, Lee and Grant, meet at the courthouse to formalize the surrender of the Confederate army. This is the climax of that horrendous conflict, the closing brief act marking and summing up the outcome. It is up to Grant, General-in-Chief of the Union Army, to decide how surrender is to play out. General Lee, a great leader who has led a smaller and less adequately equipped army that was probably destined to eventual defeat, comes to the meeting not knowing exactly what to expect. Perhaps he is dreading the humiliation.

What happens at Appomattox is extraordinary. Grant graciously treats Lee with utmost respect, provides ample food to the starving Confederate forces, and sends them home with their horses so they can resume their farming and feed their families. The Union troops are allowed no celebration. Grant orders the firing of victory salutes stopped. "The war is over," he tells his staff. "The rebels are our countrymen again."

Where do gestures of such goodness and grace come from? What is there about us that makes it possible for us to act with such sensitivity and regard for someone? Grant was certainly not a man without personal flaws. His judgment was sometimes very poor. He was naïve about the unscrupulous motivations of many whom he allowed to influence him. He drank excessively. But his actions were often richly flavored with the same goodness and grace we see at Appomattox. At a time when he could have indulged himself, if even subtly, in lording it over his adversaries, he acted with care and compassion.

I believe goodness is in our nature, as flawed as that nature is. It is true that people we consider good sometimes do bad things. The Bible is replete with examples. At the same time, people we consider bad sometimes do good things, seemingly in spite of their prominent flaws. The Bible also has some examples of this. Within all of us there is a goodness and grace waiting to emerge, ready to grow us toward who we are created to be. This goodness and grace is God's gift. He calls us to his likeness. This is our destiny in his image. We would do well, then, to turn our attention to God. Who is this God who creates us to be like him?

God in Himself

If God is good and gracious, he is free to follow his heart. Goodness and grace flow from genuine love, and love is genuine only if it is freely given. It can never be controlled or extracted exactly as we specify. The love of God is therefore a gift in which to delight, which appears unexpectedly, often like a jack-in-the-box popping up to the squealing joy of a child. The surprise of God's love keeps us slightly off balance. We cannot predict or control this God; nor can we manipulate him to maintain the comfortable balance we wish for our lives. His goodness and grace is the free gift of his love, wonderfully unpredictable.

Do we, however, prefer to think of God in more foreseeable ways? As a concept we can understand? As a definition we can grasp? Would we prefer him conveniently wrapped in a box, as it were, rather than unpredictably free to act like the jack-in-a-box? Do we prefer he not jump outside the boundaries of how we have defined him and how we expect him to act? We might prefer a manageable God. Much of religion, in fact, is aimed at figuring out how we can manage him. If that seems an exaggeration, perhaps we could say it another way: Much of religion is aimed at figuring out what God wants so that we can act in such a way as to give it to him and reap the benefits of his approval. This, however, leads nowhere because it presumes we have figured out the mind of God, which of course we will never do. We cannot contain or define God, nor can we exploit him for our ends.

However, the Christian faith does say God is a person we can know. It even goes so far as to say he is a person who loves us. It says he loves us so much he will go to extraordinary lengths for us. It claims we can rely on him to follow his heart.

When I look back over my own spiritual journey, I can see myself moving closer and closer to the heart of God and further and further from the prescriptions of religion. I remember re-freshing relief when the atmosphere around me seemed redolent with God's generosity and grace, when I knew a lightness of spirit, and my own spiritual aspirations suddenly seemed like burdensome idolatry. It continues to happen, especially when I sense I am known and accepted as a person. God, I believe, is behind it all and in it all, whether I experience this love through another person or in the breakthrough of solitude. There is no accounting for what I am knowing at the time other than to compare it to what happens between persons. There is nothing calculating about it, and it certainly cannot be managed, like some ritual or prescription—I am receiving grace from the loving heart of God.

Christians speak of God as unchangeable. What does that really mean? I believe it can mean only one thing: The heart of God is steady and unchangeable in its generosity and compassion. We can count on his love. I would not say all the rest is up for grabs, but I *would* say there is much about God we cannot figure out or understand; therefore, we cannot confidently or dogmatically predict he will do this or that in any particular way at any particular time or in any particular situation. The Bible even dares to say he can change his mind. In one famous story, Abraham "convinces" God to change his mind more than once (Genesis 18:20-33). The interesting thing about this story is that God "gives in" to Abraham's sequence of pleas for Sodom because doing so would allow people to live. In another story God is grieved as his angel is meting out punishment on Israel because of King David's disobedience. The punishment has been decided by God, but his heart suddenly cannot bear to continue and he suddenly orders his angel to stop (I Chronicles 21:1-15). In stories like these, God seems to permit his heart to change his mind.

The confidence with which we pray and bring our requests to God is not the assurance that God will do a *particular* thing if we ask him in faith. The name-it-and-claim-it approach to prayer, at best, assumes we know exactly what God wants and how he is going to do it and, at worst, is an arrogant attempt to treat God as a personal servant at our beck and call. (In the story of Abraham's pleading with God for God to spare the city, there is only the naming of a request. There is no evidence of Abraham claiming beforehand.) Rather, the confidence with which we pray is confidence in God's unmerited favor and goodness. The way in which he responds to our prayers is the way of his love. This love may express itself in a way different from the particular thing we are asking. God's love has a wisdom and a long view that we know little or nothing about. What we can be confident of, though we may not see or understand it at the time, is that God's love is the driving force and can ultimately be trusted.

One could argue that this understanding ignores the greatness of God. It suggests God cannot make up his mind and does not have the ability to respond to our requests when we make them. It makes God seem to be, well, unreliable and imperfect.

Let us talk about the idea of God's perfection. It is another idea borrowed from Greek philosophy (and especially Plato) rather than found in scripture. In its most characteristic passages, scripture gives witness to a God of extraordinary goodness and grace. Plato and his disciples give witness to a perfect God made necessary by a philosophy that says there must be a perfect reality that embodies the virtues so meagerly demonstrated by humans. Plato sees this reality as absolute goodness and justice, the perfect expression of what we humans achieve only inconsistently. In this view our calling as humans is to move closer and closer to this absolute perfection by perfecting our souls. God, this absolute perfection, is not really a person but an idea or ideal to which the moral person is drawn.

God as absolute perfection tends to make us continually aware of our imperfection and emphasize our distance from "him." (I put "him" in quotations because the God we have in this view is not truly a person.) Furthermore, it contradicts the Christian claim that in Jesus God became flesh (i.e., entered our world of imperfection) and interacted with us on our level. The Apostle Paul rightly observed that the Christian gospel was foolishness to the Greeks. Yet Platonism has found its way into the thinking of many Christians over these two thousand years. Many think of God as absolute perfection (how, then, could he possibly understand *us?*), or as the unmoved mover (how can any real person, even God the person, be this?). Such views, while they seem to honor the greatness of God, make him inaccessible to us. They use language that is foreign to scripture, ideas borrowed by the church under the influence of philosophy. Such language paints a picture of a God with whom I cannot interact and who cannot help me. He can only be an ideal toward which I can aspire, but he cannot love me, nor I him. This is not the God whom the Bible describes with ever-increasing clarity and growing certainty.

When we come to the realization that God is a person, the whole idea of the unmoved mover makes little or no sense. When we realize further that he wants fellowship with us, becomes one of us in Jesus, and lives in the world through his Spirit, the idea of his absolute, inaccessible perfection also makes no sense. When we say God is a person, we are saying he is not confined or bound by our borders, nor that his nature requires that he act in one particular way—unless, of course, that way is love. He does not sit immobile on some throne, pulling strings or meting out judgment. He lives where all real persons must live—in a story, not in a concept.

God in His Story

All persons have stories; in fact, each of us *is* a story. That is why stories permeate the Bible, each of which forms part of a larger story, the story of God and his interaction with us.

The Bible is the story of God. It is not only a story to be heard or read but a story we are invited to enter. The Bible seems more interested in stories that draw us in than in ideas that expand our minds. Perhaps this is because while good ideas may help to improve our thinking, good stories can transform our lives. In his book *A Christianity Worth Believing*, Doug Pagitt tells about his conversion to Christian faith as a sixteen-year-old. He had been raised with almost no religious influence, much less knowledge of the Christian gospel. A friend who was a new Christian invited him to a Passion Play. Doug totally misunderstood what a Passion Play was; he did not think it had anything to do with religion. He agreed to go with his friend only because of that misunderstanding! What he saw in the play was not at all what he expected. The story Pagitt witnessed became an explosive revelation that began a radical transformation of his life. At this stage in his journey, Doug had developed only a vague sense of God. The closest thing he knew about how God might be at work in the world was a TV character called Billy Jack, his hero who stood up for the powerless. Before his eyes, he was now seeing the real story. He found himself powerfully drawn to this Jesus: the kindness; the compassion, especially for the weak; the suffering; the death; the Resurrection—the whole story. When the appeal was given for those who were ready to give their lives to this Jesus, he jumped to his feet and practically ran to the stage.

Then he was led backstage and introduced to someone's *analysis* of what had happened on stage, presented as concepts the acceptance of which was the way to salvation. It totally confused him, or at least he could not connect the concepts with the story he had just witnessed on stage. It was as if he was being asked to accept this analysis of what had been depicted on stage as more important than what had actually happened. He had been drawn to the story of Jesus, and now he was being pressured to accept doctrinal bullet points. The story itself was being ignored. Unfortunately, young Pagitt's experience is not atypical. The Christian Church has all too often reduced the gospel to simplistic bullet points and missed the richness of the story the gospel invites us to enter.

The Bible is a book of stories worth telling. The Old Testament teaches us to tell the stories of God's goodness and grace to our children so that the life-changing events of God's dealings with our ancestors in the faith can continue to inspire and transform (Deuteronomy 4:9). The New Testament centers on the story of Jesus and the stories of his disciples, inviting us to come and follow, to join the story. The heart and source of all the theology and teaching in the Bible is the story, the story of God and the world, the story the Bible invites us to enter.

When God commands Abram of Haran to pull up stakes, he is leading him into a new story of promise. When he speaks to Moses from a burning bush, he is inviting this fugitive to partner with him in a new chapter in the story: leading Hebrew slaves into the freedom of the Promised Land. The stories continue over the ensuing centuries as God invites his people to new chapters. As we read the progression of the story, we realize that much of it is actually the regression of a people. The story is full of pitfalls and failures as the people again and again step outside the story into which God has invited them and construct their own story, apart from God, which turns out to be a distortion of reality, like some cheap fiction. The kings of Judah and Israel, with only a few exceptions, get drunk on power and pursue the false stories of other gods who endorse their ambitions and help them write a storyline that honors power over morality. Most people in the nation follow suit and decide to live in this story that is a lie. Prophets appear on the scene to remind the people of God that they are created and called to live in God's story, but the people mostly choose the other story, the lie that promises returns that always prove empty and in the end contaminate their soul.

Then God narrows down his own story to one human being, the man Jesus. Now the story of God becomes the story of this one person, this Aramaic Jew who lives only thirty-three years. He begins an itinerate ministry at age thirty and is executed three years later. This is not a *success story*; it is a *saving story*. It is the story of God's radical goodness and generosity, pouring into human history, reaching critical mass in Jesus' suffering and death for the salvation of the human race. The story lives on in his disciples whose own stories come to reside in this gospel story, this story of God now with us. What these Christ-followers come to see and believe is that in Jesus, God was present in a way never seen before. He was in Jesus to carry out a transformative mission. "In Christ'" says the Apostle Paul, "God was reconciling the world to himself" (II Corinthians 5:19a NRSV). Christians are people who not only believe this story but allow themselves to be claimed and changed by it. They live in it.

Living in God's Story

What is it like to live in God's story? It is allowing ourselves to be claimed by the narrative of God's generosity and grace. It is letting the story of a loving God so permeate our being we are both transformed and empowered by it. It is no longer to hide behind the lie of our insignificance and powerlessness, and instead, to risk the courage of a compassionate life. It is accepting the frightening fact that our lives, as small as we may feel in what seems to us a world of irresistible contrary forces, have a strange, quiet power God gives us, the power to give up our desperate, ego-centered lives, and receive the gift of generosity and grace. This is the power he reveals to us in the story of Jesus. Jesus, the man who gives up power—and in this most powerful of all acts, shows us the power of love. This is the realm we enter when we walk our way into God's story with our own stories, and allow God's story to grace ours with a plot and a purpose worth living and dying for.

Living in God's story or, in Jesus' vision—entering the kingdom of God—is not simply a matter of making some kind of easy change, like switching political parties, or team loyalty, or jobs. It is a matter of changing our hearts, which is a way of describing *a conversion*, a radical reorientation of our lives, and it begins with an acknowledgment that the false story we have been living has often been a betrayal of our true humanity. It is no easy thing to admit that much of one's life has been the pursuit of a fantasy that has led nowhere. It is no easy thing to allow ourselves to see that whatever importance we have ascribed to our proud accomplishments, most of them neither fulfill nor ennoble us. Confessing this fact is the necessary first step to starting a new story. We must recognize the old story is not worth living in, because our obsession with greatness only diminishes us. When we come to this threshold, we may be ready to embark on a different course, away from our addiction to more and more and toward the freedom of less and less. Living in God's story will turn us away from our desperate climb toward bigger things and rescript us in our new role, a descent into the greater worth of smaller things. There the God who became small awaits us. There he invites us to search our souls and claim our true humanity.

Centering our lives on the smaller, more personal dimensions of life can free us to live out of the integrity of our own heart and soul. Opening ourselves to the small people, small places, small moments, and small matters of our lives puts us in touch with our true selves. Seeing God in the little things, as Margaret Moore did when an African child wandered into her day and brought some tender clarity, connects us with who we are in God's presence rather than who we desperately aspire to be in our autobiographies.

To live fully in our small world is to prepare ourselves to live with generous grace and moral courage in the larger world empowered to reject one of the greatest threats to our humanity: fear. One of the most puzzling incongruities of our enlightened world has been a stubborn persistence of the process by which religious and cultural diversity within a society is fabricated into a rationale for fearing and hating. By now we should know better. Still today, groups that might be identified as different from us are made into either implicit or explicit enemies that can undermine our way of life or threaten us in some other way. Crafted by fear, such narratives become horror stories.

Freeing the African slaves of the pre–Civil War South was seen as a potential threat to the southern way of life and the fabric of its economic system. Consequently, the egregious system of slavery was strictly enforced, often with the cruelest and most violent methods. Undergirding the charm and gentility of life in

Dixie was systemic cruelty and oppression. The fear of losing a coveted way of life combined with a racist fear of the black man turned into a hatred that made the African race a threat that had to be suppressed either with condescending kindness or harsh abuse. The few close and caring relationships that did develop between whites and slaves were all the more exceptional because of the culture that fed into a fear of the black man, which was foundational to maintaining this social system and to the preservation of the wealthy and the plantation system. This fear-based racism became normative on a large scale in the years that followed, institutionalized and enforced through laws in the South, more insidious and yet still eruptive in other parts of the country. People who were otherwise respectable and decent gave in to an irrational fear perpetuated on a large scale, whether overtly or covertly, and with Jim Crow this racism became an acceptable part of society.

It is not difficult to name contemporary instances of degrading attitudes and immoral actions toward groups that are identified as different by virtue of race, culture, or creed. Often, the hatred is two-way. Groups hate each other, spread lies about each other, and commit heinous crimes against each other. No continent on earth is exempted from the scourge. It is a social curse that, when seemingly resolved by some reconciliation, simply lies dormant, only to re-emerge when fear has its way again. What seems to make this plague possible is the surrender of personal morality to the force of the fear that grips an entire community, and when the fear is generalized in this way, it crafts a moral justification for the hatred that ensues. A compassionate morality cannot thrive where moral attitudes are controlled by deep suspicion of others.

Nelson Mandela is a true hero of our times. One of the most important secrets of his moral power is his refusal to give in to the fear-based attitudes of the majority. Mandela stood firm against the racism of white South Africans who lived in a narrative of suspicion toward black South Africans and crafted a lie of racial inferiority to justify apartheid. Mandela refused to live in this fiction. Then, once political freedom had been achieved and Mandela himself was President of South Africa, many of his black supporters and associates urged the exclusion of whites from positions of influence in his government: Whites could not be trusted to work alongside the leaders of the new South Africa. Mandela also refused to live in this reverse fiction. He knew most whites expected the exclusion. Had most of them not done the same when they controlled the country? Mandela's strategy was different. He restrained the temptation toward retribution and surprised whites with his generous inclusion. I imagine this courageous morality, this miracle of generosity and grace, grew in his soul over the many years of his imprisonment in the small world of Robbin's Island, where the universe of his life was a cell, a small inner court, and the rock quarry where he broke stones daily under the watch of armed guards. That place, those many years, those fellow prisoners were a small space where he learned to transcend the lies and find in his heart the grace to trust compassion and dispel fear. The private, small world he cultivated on Robbin's Island so possessed him that he did not flinch in the face of pressure to choose the low road of moral compromise once he eventually obtained political power.

What does all this have to do with how we see God? What does it have to do with our humanity? I believe the bigger we make God, the easier it is to see him as either endorsing or turning a blind eye to our immoralities. We do not see him as relating to us as individuals, as persons, but rather as humanity, overall, just as our removal from the life of another person encourages us to see him solely, for example, as a fundamentalist Muslim, a Jew, a black man, a liberal, a fundamentalist Christian, and so the list goes. When we change the relationship from a broad category to one-on-one, interpersonal connection, when we allow ourselves to get small and engage with another person apart from the herd stereotype we may be tempted to lay on him, we become capable of love. We are able to be gracious and generous. This is morality from within rather than from without.

Jacob Needleman refers to immorality-in-the-guise-of-morality as "herd morality" (2007, 203). Giving in to fear, we suppress our own moral instincts and conform to the fear. Or, if our moral instincts are not yet well formed, we may uncritically believe the herd is right. At worst, the precepts of herd morality are harmfully immoral. At best, they are merely trivial and superficial. In all cases, to the extent we substitute the herd morality for deeply held moral convictions, and herd behavior for moral action motivated by compassion and fairness, we have lived outside God's story.

Herd morality goes beyond the more abhorrent expressions of racial, ethnic, and religious prejudice. It can be far more subtle and seemingly harmless, much easier for us to justify. When discrimination against a certain group of people is inscribed in the law of a nation, it can easily be seen as morally acceptable. When it is endorsed by a fundamentalist religion, it is seen as holy. When it is institutional policy, it is accepted as the status quo. An example I am familiar with is when employees at a lower level are given less medical benefits than those enjoyed by employees in higher positions. I once objected to such disparity in health benefits only to give up too easily when I was shown data proving the organization's resources could not support parity in the matter. To my shame, I gave in to something that was seen as normal, acceptable, and necessary but that I could not justify morally.

There are countless compromises of this kind in the world. The temptation is to accept them as normal and justifiable and not let them bother us. Certainly we should actively oppose situations where people are being abused. When it comes to the multitude of inequities that abound, however, we do not have the physical and emotional energy to address them all, and if we tried we would exhaust ourselves to the point of ineffectiveness. Margaret Moore's honesty about the compromises she had to make with a racist government in Rhodesia (as she called them, "my own betrayals") in order to be there as an influence for a more hopeful future, are testimony not only to her human fallibility but also to her deep integrity.

Frankly, the herd morality is overwhelming. At worst, it serves to disarm our moral sensitivities and make our non-caring acceptable. At best, it challenges us to confess our own imperfections and disavow ridiculously false claims to our own moral perfection. It then invites us to live our lives more fully by cultivating the compassion that shapes a true humanity. We can discover this compassion deep within us, awaiting the courage to express itself through action that refuses to accept the herd morality as the outline of our story and the arbiter for our actions. However, we are often a lone voice and may feel overwhelmed by the herd, and accused by our own compromises. We are aware of our weaknesses and wonder if we are just trying to be difficult. Do we really want our lives to be a story unlike the script the herd is following? Do we have the courage?

And then we learn that this script the herd is following is not a true story at all but a fabrication. It is an invention of a society that has lost its way and is trying to build a life that pretends it has not. It is a story without substance and therefore no real story at all. It goes nowhere.

There is only one real story, and it is the story of God. There is only one way my own story can be real, and that is for me to enter God's story of generosity and grace. God's story puts me in touch with my soul, the heart of who I am: a creation of God put together for compassion. Compassion is not an abstraction. It is live action played out in my story, released with courage because I now live in God's story where loving others is *normal*. Jesus summed up this way of living in what he called the first and second greatest commandments: "You must love the Lord your God with all your heart, with all your being, and with all your mind" and "You must love your neighbor as you love yourself" (Matthew 22:37-39).

God challenges us to find our true humanity in an attitude of generosity and grace and through acts of compassion. This humanity is not found in the world of ideas. It cannot be legislated by decree. It cannot be mastered by force of will. It is a gift given by our Creator, who invites us to live in his story and watch his love at work in the small world of our lives.

Yes, we must live fully in the small world of our lives, or we will never know love. Whoever we are, whatever our so-called status in the world-at-large or in the community in which we live, we will find our way only by giving primary attention to our small world. We will only get lost in the larger world that follows the herd and requires we surrender our souls. This is true even for those who have leadership responsibilities that affect large numbers of people or head large organizations or government bodies—people who are viewed as living on a large scale in a world that cannot be bothered by smaller matters. If we cannot live with generosity and grace in our small world—the world of our family and friends, the intimate places of personal significance, the remembered experiences of personal transformation, the times when someone reaches out to us or we to them—no matter what our place in the social order, we shall live in captivity to the lost herd and never really find our way. Herds are too big for stories and too afraid for love.

Authentic life begins in a small world. Whether this truth is discovered in our early years or later in life, life unfolds when our souls are being formed, our hearts are being purified, and our lives are starting to receive the gift of generosity and grace. To stray from these beginnings, to surrender integrity for the compromises of the herd and be captive to fear is a sure way to sell our souls. We become someone we are not; our stories become mere fiction. David the shepherd becomes David the king who overreaches; the integrity of his small beginnings is abandoned for triumph and a lust for more. His fall from grace is hardly an isolated case in the course of human history; it is characteristic of our grasping ways.

I dare say every one of us has met with such failure at one time or another as we have navigated, sometimes more successfully than others, the strong currents of this temptation: to be so drawn to the seductive scrambling for more for ourselves, a desperate pursuit driven by trusting fear over love. Our chase for more makes us forget the small world of our true loves. To find our way we must return to our beginnings.

William Booth was co-founder with his wife Catherine of a movement that invaded the world of poverty and systemic human abuse with the message of a loving God and a ministry of compassion. The movement became known as The Salvation Army. Where did this story begin? When asked about it, William would usually answer by saying it began in a church in Nottingham, England, where as a lad of fifteen he decided that "God would have all there is of William Booth." This was the seemingly insignificant time and place when young William entered God's story, and, to the best of his ability, he stayed there for the rest of his life. Later, after William had served as a Methodist minister for a number of years, he and Catherine made the difficult decision to leave the denomination, because its leaders refused to honor his calling to the unchurched poor and insisted William take another circuit. Over time the Booths found themselves in the poorest part of London, the East End, where William said he "got the poor of London on his heart" and concluded he had found his destiny." And so, another chapter of their story began. The story unfolded in one place after another where those considered small people lived their lives, until this army for the forgotten was planted around the world. William Booth was not a perfect man, but he stayed on the course set out for him at his beginning; he never forgot the day he decided to live in the overwhelming reality of God's story, never forgot the generosity and grace of God.

If life truly begins in a small world, so there does it end. When we consider the end of our lives on earth, we may well assume we will want, above all, to depart with some pride in our accomplishments. We may think this is the legacy we want to leave behind, the thing for which we want to be remembered. I suspect this may prove not to be as important as we may think. In fact, it may shrink to relative insignificance. As our earthly life nears its end, I think we will treasure the memories of intimate moments, the joy of loving, the small matters that will then seem so large, so important—the community of relationships that have helped to shape us and the persons for whom we have been able to be mentors and models, the opportunities we have had to share compassion with another person, and the deep sense of knowing God's blessing. If we cannot bring these to our final days, we die impoverished in spirit. If we can, we have experienced the fulfillment of living in the story of God's generosity and grace. We have found what we were meant to do and, more important, who we were meant to be.

part 4

Following God
to
the Freedom
of the Small

Seven

Letting the Subversive Gospel Turn Us and Our Values Upside Down

THE CHRISTIAN GOSPEL is a subversive creed in a culture of unrepressed, self-seeking individualism. It is a dangerous threat to the compromises and power of all human herds. Jesus' teaching that the first will be last and the last first does not commend itself to people who are trying very hard to get ahead or stay ahead of everyone else (Matthew 20:16). Nor does his frequent disregard for generally accepted social values commend him to the complacent. I doubt, for example, his admonishment to forgive without limit someone who sins against you again and again was generally accepted practice (Matthew 18:21-22). Nor that his parable about the so-called dregs of humanity in the street being invited to the banquet of God's Kingdom endeared him to the well-heeled people on the original guest list who were too preoccupied or proud to respond (Matthew 14:15-24).

It should come as no surprise that people of all sorts had mixed feelings about Jesus. The politicians and government representatives were intrigued by the magnetism and popular appeal of this man. But they were afraid his teachings about the kingdom of God where all classes of people were fully accepted might become an ideology spurring popular insurrections. It was no accident the Roman Empire's system of capital punishment was ultimately the means of eliminating the threat of Jesus. The religious leaders were amazed by this carpenter-rabbi's grasp of scripture and his appeal to the common people. But they were threatened by his audacity in going further than the law, his presumption in speaking of God in intimate, familiar terms, and his blatant attack against their corruption of Jewish faith. It was not surprising they marshaled their religious authority and manipulated their own Sanhedrin court to deliver a ruling of blasphemy, a sentence deserving of death according to their laws. The masses of common people "listened to him with delight" (Mark 12:37). They loved his deep connection with their lives and their suffering; they were drawn to his Kingdom that honored their small world; and they enjoyed his willingness to poke fun at the people in power. But they wanted something concrete to happen to improve their situation. Many of them wanted revenge against the powerful people who exploited them. Since Jesus' kingdom was "not from this world" and the very nature of it prevented the use of violent means to achieve its ends, in Jesus' final days the masses did not come to his aid. Some of them allowed their disillusionment to turn into cruel revenge against him (John 18:36 NRSV).

At the time none of these groups were ready to receive the message and live the life to which Jesus was calling them. They were in captivity to a way of thinking they thought best served their interests, and they would have wanted this Jesus to support it. We should go easy on them, as they are so much like us. We, like they, want meaning. We want a life that has value, and we want to be valued. We want to understand who we are and what we can believe in and live for.

When, however, we allow prevailing cultural values to shape us, the mass media to define us, and the herd to direct us, we give up the possibility of freedom and largely define ourselves by fear of being different, fear of disapproval, and fear of exclusion. Ironically, many see Christians as largely motivated by these same fears. Indeed, some who claim the Christian faith are. They have made Jesus the idol of their status quo, the protector of their life-style, the lover of their success, or the guarantor of their desperate hopes for the future. Whether they have realized the American Dream or are still hoping to find it, they have intentionally opted for a gospel that is rightside-up with their culture. It is quite possible they simply do not know anything else is possible.

The gospel of Jesus is at odds with our dominant Western culture, even much of our church culture. This is because it inverts our sense of what is important. It calls us to the freedom of the small. It calls us to give attention to the all-important unimportant, the all-important here and now, and the all-important, vulnerable people, including ourselves. It calls us to see reality, to live attentively, to resist the distraction of self-aggrandizement, and with open hearts to receive the presence of God and of those he brings our way.

Gospel Inversion: The All-Important Unimportant

Harvard professor and scholar of the Hebrew Bible James L. Kugel battled cancer for several years. He testified that this difficult journey helped him to see. The dark valley he passed through pushed him to reassess his faith. He found himself feeling small, his world shrinking. "It is not God's sovereignty over the entire universe that is at issue," he writes, "as much as his sovereignty over the cubic centimeter of space that sits just in front of our own noses" (Shulevitz 2011, 22). When something intervenes to confront us with the reality of our mortality, the unimportant becomes all-important, the small large. Our death, in fact, is the ultimate wake-up call to our smallness. Perhaps that is why and how it is a gift. It helps us claim and treasure the small things that suddenly now seem so important and enduring.

I want to be clear about what I mean. First, let me clarify what I am *not* saying. The all-important unimportant things are not thoughtless trivialities. They are not boredoms in which we allow ourselves to be trapped nor the distractions that disconnect us. They are not things done poorly that deserve to be forgotten, whether those things be on a small or a large scale. They are not trivial pursuits and shallow acts. The all-important unimportant are moments of surprising grace and beauty. They are also the simple gestures that reveal love; the spontaneous kindnesses that have the sweet aroma of mercy; the respectful confrontations, private and public, that nurture integrity and clarity; and the service done in quiet humility. They are the small acts of genuine attentiveness and compassion.

Compassion cannot be marketed. Sometimes the story of a simple act of kindness, an act that was humbly performed in love, catches the imagination when it becomes well known. At some point someone gets the idea of promoting similar acts of kindness to encourage others to follow suit. A campaign is launched to help people discover the joy of these experiences by duplicating them in their own settings. Soon the simple act has become a program. Such promotions of a good act can encourage people to take first steps toward living their own lives compassionately. They can also morph into gestures motivated by making ourselves feel morally acceptable, and therefore such gestures are simply a duty to be over and done with. The spontaneous kindness can become a legalistic compulsion, compassion a prescription.

In the Western world, most people live in large cities where neighborhoods are most often formed and defined by socio-economic levels and personal interests. People typically confine themselves to their worlds of family and friends, workplace, immediate neighborhood, and recreation. The large majority of the marginalized, therefore, exist in isolated and sometimes relatively inaccessible pockets. Consequently, help and needed support has been delegated to specialized community service organizations funded by private donations, foundation grants, and government allocations. Service is dispensed within the clearly defined requirements of policy and guidelines. While acts of genuine caring can and do take place within such arrangements, this confinement of compassion raises some important questions about how we are living. Does this situation discourage us from our calling as human beings in the image of God to reach out to others in need? (Deuteronomy 15:7-11; Proverbs 14:21,31; 28:27; 31:8-9; Matthew 25:31-45). Does this arrangement encourage us to opt for our compassion to be delegated? And *can* compassion be delegated?

Many people give to such service agencies—some very generously. Without that support, many more needs would go unmet. Yet I wonder how many reckon their financial contribution excuses them from allowing themselves to be face-to-face with the hurting and suffering of others. The word *compassion* means "to suffer with someone." Charitable giving may or may not be motivated by compassion. It may be that the giver cannot realistically be involved with the marginalized community his contribution is helping. The giver can, however, be attentive to those who are near. In that small place, he or she can enter the suffering of others as well as their joy. In this way, the giver finds in that participation the full reward of his or her own humanity in God's image, which delegated giving can only bring in small measure.

Compassion is not a funded program, though it can be expressed through giving in such a manner and setting. Compassion is someone acting in humility to share generosity and grace with another person. Compassion is, at times, having little to give but a full heart to share. Compassion is the humble, self-emptying act of being with someone who is at a low point or who lives in a low place. Compassion finds those seen as unimportant and makes them all-important.

Compassion also senses there are deep matters beneath the surface of the person before us and pauses to honor, name, and receive the moment. I am a task-oriented person. My mother used to tell me that as a child I always seemed to have some project going. I am a beaver that loves to stay busy with a plan. This is an important part of who I am. There is another side to me, as there is to all of us. It is this willingness to be genuinely attentive to another person, this ability to listen and care. I do think we all have this side to us, and, in fact, it is more than a side; it is at the heart of who we are in God's image. Some people seem to have attentive personalities that make it easier for them to stop what they are doing and make themselves available to another person. As for me, I sometimes have to give my preoccupied self permission to stop and step aside, give myself fully to the person before me, and offer my gift of compassion to them, which also is a gift to me. I find that when I do this—or better still, when I *am* this—I sense God is present in some way, inviting me to receive the moment and this person as his gift, as he is inviting the other person to receive me. Something happens I cannot quite put my finger on other than to say in those times I am at peace with who I am in a deeper way than I am when I am supposedly accomplishing something. I am a person created in the image of God to receive and reflect his generosity and grace. Everything else I enjoy doing is also a part of who I am, but this caring is at the core of my humanity. Without it I am empty at my center.

I believe God is calling us all to live in this way, to find our humanity in the inversion that is compassion. Compassion is not an occasional attitude of our heart precipitated by a moving story or an emotional appeal. It is a state of being. It is a permanently subversive condition of rebellion against a self-seeking world. We do not cease being compassionate today because we have been sufficiently compassionate in the past. We do not postpone compassion today because we plan to get serious about it in the future. Compassion is neither occasional nor convenient. It is not put aside for any reason of accommodation or compromise. It is woven into the fabric of who we are, and it lives in the all-important now.

Inversion Living: The All-Important Now

The pursuit of more and more removes us from the present moment. We spend our days either dreaming of the future prosperity for which we long or planning to make it happen. Dreaming of and planning for tomorrow are not bad things. Our dreams open our minds to new possibilities, and our planning is the first step to making our dreams a reality. However, when we live in a continuous state of dissatisfaction with who we are and what we have, and when our minds are forever distracted by the unknown future, we have robbed ourselves of the day.

In chapter 5 we spoke of the noonday demon of acedia. Acedia immobilizes us with doubt about the significance of the moment. It paralyzes us with an emptiness that finds nothing of value in the hours that pass. It renders us unable to live in the fullness of the now.

Perhaps much of religion, including Christianity, contributes to this by drawing lines too bold or facile between sacred and secular. In such a scheme, the times we think of as sacred are those when we pay attention to God and perhaps even connect in some way with him. Secular times are when we are on our own. According to this distinction, the great majority of us spend most of our time in the secular world. In the secular world, it is understood that different rules apply. We are about the business of making a living and working hard to build better lives for ourselves and our families, having fun, and enjoying friends. We are not exactly being holy, or at least we do not see this as a primary concern in the secular realm of our lives. We are not paying particular attention to what may lie beneath the surface. We are not expecting something surprising to jump out from our routines. We do not expect to encounter God, and therefore we usually do not.

What if this way of living out our days is profoundly misguided? What if it impoverishes our lives? What if it causes us to miss the fullness of the moment? I suspect most of us know in our hearts that it does. I certainly do. I can think back to times when I was too preoccupied to connect with something significant, too busy to be surprised by unexpected grace, too intent to notice the inner cry of another person, or of myself. These missed moments are, I believe, moments of breakthrough I was not ready to receive. My attention was elsewhere.

I am afraid our fast-paced world is robbing us of the blessings of the now. Pausing and paying attention are not high values in our social settings. Moving fast and keeping up with the latest technology, app, entertainment, or job opportunity makes it very difficult for us to stop, listen, and look into who or what is speaking to our souls. Perhaps we are willing conspirators in it all. We may keep ourselves distracted because we fear allowing the significance of the all-important now to enter our hearts.

I am increasingly convinced social media, which on the surface seems and claims to make us more connected and attentive to each other, is actually accomplishing the opposite. It is undeniable that social media can be used to express and facilitate compassion. At the same time we must realize that immediacy is not the same as intimacy. Accessibility is not the same as attentiveness. Intimacy requires a strong self-awareness that is the fruit of solitude, self-examination, and a history of face-to-face encounters. Intimacy is not nurtured through the ever-present externalized feedback and the resulting self-image-crafting that rapidly occurs on Facebook and Twitter. True attentiveness is certainly not deeply fostered by the ongoing scrolls of messages in which the minute details of life are shared. Too often in these messages, the publicizing becomes hype and the concern peaks fast and then recedes. There is little opportunity to pause over the important matters of someone's journey because the messaging floods in at a rapid rate. Is it truly possible to process matters of real depth in the fast-moving world of the social network?

There have always been ways to shield ourselves from an awareness of others and to avoid being attentive to the people near us. I think we have reached a new level of potential insensitivity. Consider how cell phones and smartphones are frequently used. These little hand-held devices create a powerful, invisible force field around us that excuse us from typical cultural and social mores and expectations, as well as interaction with others. Cell phones grant upon us a degree of entitlement and a pass to ignore not only the least of these but, at times, friends and family. The smartphone is even more subtle: on it we can not only text silently but search the Internet to occupy our time and keep from interacting with those who are often right in front of us. Sadly, cell phone and smartphone use begins at a very early age. Children are learning they can live their lives largely on the Internet and the opportunity to practice and enjoy face-to-face interaction is decreased. I know people who resist using even the telephone. They will almost always e-mail or text, and I strongly suspect it is because the telephone is only one step away from face to face and is therefore more personal and demanding for them. They choose, or may feel pressured, to exist on the Internet, as if their life is not real until it appears there. A recent cartoon of Mike Luckovich depicted this state of affairs with humor, but also with implicit sadness. A priest performs a wedding. He says, "You may kiss the bride," while at the same time he Tweets: "Telling groom to kiss bride." Also at the same time the groom is Tweeting, "Kissing bride," while the bride is Tweeting, "Getting kissed." Not to be left out of the social network, each member of the congregation is Tweeting "Watching kiss" (2011, A18).

Ironically, the social network is being preempted by our lust for more and more. We use it not to help us be more attentive to one another but only more aware of the minute details of the ever-expanding matrix of our social media friends and followers. Instead of bringing us closer it would be more accurate to say these high-tech interactions only keep us informed. Such a platform creates an incessant need for constant information that can never be enough. It keeps our minds and our fingers moving to capture the latest particulars and to keep in the know. At the same time, it teaches us to relate to one another through the sterile world of few words and images on a screen, a world without the content of real presence—genuinely seeing, feeling, touching, hearing, and savoring. The social network is not the utopia of a connected world; it is the utopia of isolated individuals who want to stay constantly in touch while not really engaging one another.

There is no need to go to the extreme and say the social network itself is demonic. It is a technology that has usefulness. Obviously, many people who live well in the all-important now also use Facebook and Twitter. They do not, however, allow it to be a substitute for their connectedness to those around them or for their openness to God's now. They understand its limits, and they do not live their lives there. They use it as a disciplined tool. The misfortune is that so many do not.

The God who created us calls us to live engaged with the world in which he has placed us. It is a world alive with the wonder and shock of God. In a society where people are scrambling to do more, do it faster, and move ahead, the powerful simplicity of the everyday world is lost. Our rush distracts us. Our drive desensitizes us. For some Christians, the Sunday morning church experience does not help. They move through the order of worship without stopping, and when it is over, they are anxious to move on and get back to reality, when reality has been staring them in the face in worship. They failed to see, hear, touch, and feel the power of the experience. Annie Dillard has sat through many church services where she concluded few connected with what was actually happening in their midst. The worshipers seemed like "brainless tourists on a packaged tour of the Absolute."

> On the whole [she writes] I do not find Christians, outside the catacombs, sufficiently sensible of the conditions. Does anyone have the foggiest idea what sort of power we so blithely invoke? Or, as I suspect, does no one believe a word of it? The churches are children playing on the floor with their chemistry sets, mixing up a batch of TNT to kill a Sunday morning. It is madness to wear ladies' straw hats and velvet hats to church; we should be wearing crash helmets. Ushers should issue life preservers and signal flares; they should lash us to our pews. For the sleeping god may awake some day and take offense, or the waking god may draw us out to where we can never return. (1982, 58–59)

Who would think that where two or three or more are gathered for timed and regulated worship on a Sunday morning, something could happen that breaks open the polite distance and prescribed etiquette, overwhelming them with awareness of God and each other (Matthew 18:20). The event that launches the Church is actually reported to have occurred in this way. It happened in a gathering of Jesus' followers and Diaspora Jews from far and near who were assembled in prayer on the day of the Jewish festival Shavuoth (Pentecost Chr). Something earth-shattering enters that small place that, over time, turns the world upside down. It is described as people being filled with the spirit of God, and this assembly of diverse people from different lands becomes so deeply aware that they understand one another despite the language barriers, and they become a very different, radically caring community (Acts 2).

Some Christians today see this event as a singular, unrepeatable occurrence, and it certainly is in the sense that it represented the birth of the Christian church after the death and resurrection of Jesus. There is much more to be said, however. Something happens here that goes beyond the startling wind and fire. There is a language spoken that everyone understands though they speak different languages. There is an outbreak of prophetic insight that the Apostle Peter says is the fulfillment of Old Testament predictions from a number of prophets. I have no idea how all this happens or what it is in detail. We only have the testimony of the Acts of the Apostles telling us God breaks into their gathering, somehow enters each of them, and the result is that they understand one another at a deeper level, they are given insight beyond the apparent, and they move toward being a truly attentive, caring community of Christ.

I think this event is a model for those who truly desire to live in the inversion of God's Kingdom, the new reality Jesus came preaching. "The kingdom of God is near," says Jesus (Mark 1:15b NIV). In fact, it is "among you" (this phrase can also be translated "within you"). Jesus is pointing to a reality seen with deep insight, not "careful observation" or facile identification (Luke 17:20-21). It surprises those who are receptive and it passes by those who are set on their way. Two years ago, our grandson Ben was still in the phase where jack-in-the-box-type surprises delighted him to no end. Once I started the game with him, we stopped only when I could play no more; he could play it forever. As he grew older and his interests became more sophisticated, he ceased to be amused by this simple game. But God forbid he becomes like those (and I have sometimes been) who want no surprises, no intrusions in life that lead to a change of some kind, no interruption of the day's plan that has been so carefully constructed, and certainly no threat to the upside world that may be defining him. Pentecost introduces those followers of Jesus to the shocking upside-down kingdom of God, and enough of them are sufficiently willing for their lives to be upended and to start a revolution. His is not a revolution that promises things around us will get better. This revolution is far more subversive, because it invites us to enter the inverted Kingdom, the radically different kingdom of God, *now*. The promise is fulfilled now for those with eyes to see and ears to hear this emerging kingdom of God in their today. And it is fulfilled for those willing to stop their rush toward tomorrow, or their pining for the past, and receive the blessing of new life in the current moment.

Living fully in the present before us makes possible our humanity. Remembering the past and learning from it is an important foundation for our humanity. Looking forward to the future with hope gives important confidence for our humanity. Receiving the day as an uncomplicated gift, expecting something profoundly important will come through an unexpected channel or an encounter with an unexpected person, provides the very opportunity for us to be who we truly are. We cannot speak of who we truly are, however, without speaking of our vulnerability.

The Inverted Kingdom: Our All-Important Vulnerability

I want to talk about two vulnerable people. The first could be any number of female tween or teen stars we may be familiar with. She may be a star of a popular TV series or a successful performer and recorder of pop music. Her public persona has probably been carefully honed, and her fans are many in number. When they see her, on screen or in person, they shout their love and devotion. Symbolically or literally, they reach out to touch her, perhaps seeking her blessing—or is it her magic?

But time has passed, and now she is on the cusp of adulthood; she is growing up. The image-makers are faced with the challenge of successfully bringing her through the transition from teen to young-adult idol. Now her attire is more suitable to starlets, her song material more "mature," her sexuality more obvious. Perhaps her image-makers have gone too far with this as she has now been criticized for some racy photos or suggestive music—after all, they are also trying to keep up with the advancing years of her fans, as well as reach an expanded adult audience. The fans are still fawning over her, following her every move, but it remains to be seen whether or not she negotiates a successful transition to adult stardom.

Frankly, while fans may know much about her carefully crafted persona, they probably know almost nothing about her true self. And she may not truly know herself, either, having invested so much in her public image, which is constantly being re-profiled to draw mature and maturing fans who will buy her brand. We have no idea how she has navigated all this. We only know what we see or hear on screen or stage, or what we read in the entertainment magazines, and this narrative allows for no flaws or inadequacies to show. She is larger than life, an idol that permits no real vulnerability, only the posed vulnerability when she is in character. The real person, of course, is genuinely vulnerable, and I suspect she may be even more vulnerable precisely because the persona she has been coached to project is an iconic house of cards that cannot finally stand. She may not know who she is behind and without the hype. She is a public image. And to the extent she tries to deal with who she really is, her true self, there will be a lot of exterior pretense she may have to bear the pain of shedding.

Perhaps she is a larger-than-life version of us all when we project an exterior self that we (or someone else) has decided is the most advantageous face for us to wear. All the while our vulnerable selves lie hidden, protected...starving for honest expression and interaction. Perhaps we feel fear and hide it behind an assumed exterior of confidence, strength, and even invincibility. Maybe we go so far as to cage ourselves into an image of who we are or think we ought to be, and whatever is happening inside us that does not fit that character is suppressed. No matter what we are feeling, if it compromises this public image it is kept hidden. We must keep the cage locked, protect whatever vulnerability revelation could expose. So we may, for example, be hurt by someone's remark but refrain from showing the pain, or we may attempt to hide such vulnerability by transforming hurt into angry reaction. Or we may honestly disagree with a course of action, but protect our acceptance or place in a group by going along and not risking having the group turn against us. We may even stand by in the face of injustice to avoid the consequences of disrupting the status quo, or to prevent placing ourselves in a vulnerable position publically. We may be more afraid of our vulnerability than we think. On the other hand, we may not.

Which brings me to another person I want to describe, a specific person. Her name was Martha. A few years ago I attended her funeral. It was one of the most moving funerals I have ever attended. One person after another gave witness to how they were better persons, and better Christians, because of what Martha had given them. Martha had died at age fifty-five, a young age to die for most. Those calculations did not apply to Martha; she had been born with Downs Syndrome. She lived a good, long life. There was reason for her health and longevity: two wonderful parents, Andy and Joan, and three siblings who cared deeply for their sister. From the very beginning Andy and Joan loved Martha and said God loved her even more. They taught her life skills and discipline, and they expected her to fulfill her share of family responsibilities. Whenever their very demanding vocations required travel, they always made sure she had a caring person with her. For Martha the world was a place of grace where love lived.

Martha's favorite song was "Jesus Loves Me." She believed it with all her heart. She called herself Jesus' girl. She liked to line up her Barbie dolls (she had quite a collection) and give each one the name of someone she knew, or someone she was aware had a problem. Every day she picked up each Barbie and prayed for the person. People excited her. Her affection for people knew no bounds. I do not know a soul who knew her who did not bask in the effusiveness of her love and often the encircling providence of her prayers.

Martha has much to teach us. She was not a larger-than-life version of who we are. She was in many ways, however, an authentic version of who we can become. With Martha, what you saw was what you got, as we say, and it carried a disarming beauty. Loved without condescension and appreciated for who she was, she lived generously with both her gifts and her limitations. She was free because she was never susceptible to the manipulations of perfectionists or image-makers. The only image she seemed to care about was God's image in her, expressed in her own tender language as Jesus' girl. She lived in that image with a pure simplicity that touched people's lives with the winsome power of it.

Some people who could not yet see may have looked upon Martha's disability as either an embarrassment or an object of pity. Here was a person who could not perform many tasks an average person could, had limited cognitive skills, and was sometimes awkward in public. Those with open eyes, however, saw a person whose unique qualities only made her more open and honest and available. The lack of pretense and affectation, the unabashed openness to love given and received, the life lived with such disarming directness, drew anyone hungering for authenticity.

Martha teaches us that in the inverted kingdom of God, where our worth is so high and we are so deeply loved, we need not be ashamed of our own vulnerabilities and limitations. Perhaps this is one reason why Jesus said we needed to become like little children to enter the Kingdom. This is the sedition of the gospel—that someone small in a vulnerable condition or place ignites something that, by the nature of it, serves to question the pretenses and oppressions of our world by demonstrating a better way to live. Those who influence through the exercise of power over others do not advance the kingdom of God. They only advance their power. Those who influence through the simple courage of their lives, the power of their compassion, and the humility of their heart release a force of love that can bring deep, lasting change. They are like yeast in the loaf, says Jesus, which quietly, subversively transforms everything around them (Luke 13:20-21).

Those who find their true humanity live with courage in the place of vulnerability. They abide with peace in the generosity and grace of a loving God. Perhaps this accounts for the undeniable effectiveness of movements to bring change through nonviolent strategies. Jesus was born in a vulnerable place, courted danger by challenging the values and power structures of religion and state, preached the power of love and condemned the love of power, and made himself vulnerable to the killing power of the Roman government. The outcome speaks for itself: an unstoppable movement of nonviolent successors who put their lives on the line, as did Jesus, because they believed perfect love casts out fear and lived and died as if it did. It is true the Church has often departed from this non-violence by using violence, in one form or another, to protect its control over matters of doctrine and morality or its political influence and wealth. It is also true that over the centuries there have been plenty of witnesses to the power of love expressed in nonviolent living—people like Francis of Assisi and thousands of others who have taken Jesus seriously. In modern times Ghandi led nonviolent protests and overthrew colonial rule. In the South, Martin Luther King Jr. led a nonviolent movement that overturned government-enforced segregation.

Nonviolence is based upon the realization that even those in the most vulnerable places have power—a very different power, to be sure—a power that calls for the greatest courage because it does not hide behind the walls of established power. It is power from within, from the center of who we are, not from what we have taken or inherited. It is the power of small.

Nonviolence is far more and deeper than a political strategy to force change. It grows from the conviction that love is more powerful than power. Nonviolent protest is protest on behalf of those whose humanity is being abused; it is an act of love. The people with the courage to do this, those who in strength and in love make themselves vulnerable to violence against them in one form or another, know at some level that love casts out fear. Love makes them servants, not subservient; strong witnesses, not helpless victims. No longer intimidated by the overwhelming odds against them, they enter the battle small, with little to show save the power of their humanity. This may not be what makes this fallen world go 'round, but it is the only thing that will keep it from destroying itself.

I believe this connects us with the inverted kingdom of God announced and taught by Jesus, the kingdom that turns our values upside-down. It comes down to the vulnerable people who accept the power of their powerlessness, the truly courageous people who seek to live in love and resist the seduction of power. It comes down to you and me, to whether we can accept the gift of vulnerability, to whether we can find love at the core of who we are, to whether we can step out from behind our worst fears and our self-protective facades and trust the power of love.

True, this kingdom of God runs up against a worldview that, while it may encourage sympathy for the marginalized or victimized, still is drawn to those at the top, those who either have been granted or have grabbed power over others. In this world, to be the weakest link is to be a pitied loser. In the kingdom of God the have-nots, the hungry, the grieved, the meek, the persecuted are blessed with God's favor (Matthew 5:3-11; Luke 6:20-22). It would be a serious mistake to think that Jesus is blessing these groups because he feels sorry for them. If there is any pity behind his words, it is for those in power who hide behind it, and use it to exploit others. It would also be a mistake to conclude Jesus is blessing the spirit and attitude of all who find themselves in poverty and marginality. Taking together all the groups he mentions, it is clear that what they have in common is the exposure of their vulnerabilities. Jesus is honoring in them the enormous possibilities of those vulnerabilities when the power of love is trusted and the love of power is not. He is saying to those openly vulnerable people that freedom is not the future prospect of power; it is the present prospect of love. The promise of a revolution that turns the tables and makes the have-nots the haves, a transfer of power from one set of hands to another, is not what Jesus is offering. He is offering what the Apostle Paul calls a "more excellent way" (NRSV), the way of love (I Corinthians 12:31b–13:1-13). The Greek word Paul uses in this important passage, translated "love" in most English versions, is the kind of love that affirms and values the other person apart from what that person can do to enhance the lover. It sees beyond how that person can give power or benefit to him. Hence, it has nothing to do with the power, prestige, or usefulness of the one loved. It has only to do with his innate beauty in the image of God, something so small by our measurements, so insignificant by our values—yet so great in the kingdom of God and so authentic when we are able and privileged to see it.

The gospel of Jesus is an uncomfortable inversion, especially to the fearful. It invites us to see our world and ourselves in a radically different way. It challenges us to question what our culture says is important and to claim the new treasure our craven pursuits have required us to diminish and devalue. It pulls us from the madness of our pace and suggests keen attentiveness to the world around us. It urges us to embrace authenticity over authority, courage over cowardice, love over fear. It calls us to fall in love with the small.

Eight

Letting Ourselves
Fall in Love
with the Small

RECENT STUDIES SHOW A DECLINE in the percentage of
Americans who call themselves Christians. I doubt it has much
to do with an increasingly thorough and objective consideration
of the life, message, and meaning of Jesus. It more likely has to do
with the perversions of Christianity, which draw media attention
or buy media time, defining the faith for the public in a way Jesus
would not recognize as his own gospel. What we have witnessed
in recent years is a glut of such counterfeits. People are turning
away from Christianity because it has been confiscated and rein-
terpreted to justify self-indulgent lifestyles, advance rigid ideologies, and polarize people for some partisan or personal advantage.
The examples range from political parties that ignorantly insist
their view of government and the common good coincides perfectly with the teaching of Jesus; to media evangelists with huge

egos who claim to represent *the* true interpretation of the Christian gospel while simultaneously building expansive empires of influence and often getting rich in the process; to people like you and me who sometimes use a shallow understanding of spirituality to condone our own shallowness. Christian faith is not losing credibility because it is being tried and found wanting. Credibility is being lost because sadly, in the name of Christianity, people are seeing, and tragically some are being hoodwinked to pursue, the wrong thing.

The non-Christian public sees professing Christians who are in love with power, who use Christianity as a tool and promote it as a way to succeed in life, in pursuit of the American Dream. Seeing this, the public either turns away disgusted or, if they are taken in, desperately embraces the same plan of seduction. Christianity is made to be the creed of bigger and better prospects in the here and now.

It is enough to make God weep, as he has surely done many times over in the face of our repeated confusion of the message of Jesus with our own self-aggrandizing ambitions. While we would like very much for God to do something big for us now, or very soon, he will not be dictated to. I think he has a different plan. I think he wants to start by turning our world upside down.

When the resurrected Jesus appears to his disciples for the last time, having already told them to wait in Jerusalem for the promised gift of the Holy Spirit, they ask him, "Lord, are you going to restore the kingdom to Israel now?" (Acts 1:6). They are eager and think they are ready for the dream of God's kingdom to become reality. They want everything fixed *now*!

The kingdom of God does not come by fiat in this way. It comes in small ways, day by day, as we discover God's generosity and grace in each other and in the world around us. It is true that Jesus sometimes speaks of the coming of God's kingdom in a future apocalypse (Matthew 24). It is the great joy and delight of all followers of Jesus to live in the sure and certain hope of the resurrection to eternal life, the full fruition of the kingdom of God in his world. In the face of future upheaval, Jesus invites his followers to "stand up straight and raise your heads, because your redemption is near" (Luke 21:28). The great weight of Jesus' teaching on the kingdom of God, however, speaks of a new reality within us, among us, hidden like a small seed or a lost coin or a buried treasure. This lost reality, this buried treasure, is now to be found and celebrated. This little seed is to be planted and nurtured, first and foremost in our own lives and in our relationships in the world as well.

It is no wonder that following the coming of the Holy Spirit to seekers gathered in the upper room (Acts 2) we find the disciples and new believers in the gospel claiming this new reality for themselves and for their life together. They start meeting together, sharing prayer, fellowship, food, and possessions. They discover the grace of God and the life of the new kingdom of God with and through each other (Acts 2:42-47). It goes even further: They turn their attention to the people they rub shoulders with every day beyond their inner circle, including and especially the poor, the marginalized, and the sick, bringing the blessing of Christ, the ministry of presence, and the seeds of change. It is probably not by accident that the apocalyptic words of Jesus in Matthew 24 referred to above are followed in chapter 25 by the famous parable of the Last Judgment. In this parable the Son of Man, Christ, invites into his eternal joy those who have fed the hungry, welcomed the stranger, clothed the naked, visited the sick, and come to the prisoner (Matthew 25:31-46). It is not surprising, then, that throughout the Acts of the Apostles we see Jesus' disciples spreading the truth that something good and new has happened, a new day has dawned, a new reality is here—*for everyone!* This was the day they had been waiting for, and it was far different and better, and more inclusive, than they had anticipated!

We have been describing this new reality in different ways throughout the course of this book. We have spoken of our small-becoming God who refuses to be kept at a cold distance, the God alongside us who is concerned about and involved in the everyday world of our lives, no matter who we are. Such a God, we have seen, invites us to live our days in his presence, receiving the gift of his generosity and grace. He calls us away from our foolish obsession with our self-enhancement, our soul-destructive drive to the top, our selling ourselves to success. We have learned how he frees us to treasure the small things, which are his greatest gifts. He is the God of small things: small people, small places, small moments, small matters. He invites us to find our story in his story, to live every day in companionship with him and with those people and in that world he blesses us with. We have also faced the seditious nature of the gospel of grace in a world craving for more and clawing for advantage, a gospel content with less and at peace with love's vulnerability. How then are we to live if we choose to take this gospel seriously and allow it to claim us and change our lives? We do what those early disciples did: We fall in love.

Falling in Love

This phrase is typically used to describe the emotional intensity of our strong attraction to another person, a state often rendering us vulnerable. To a certain extent this description suitably describes the person who is attracted to Jesus. Jesus has a magnetism that draws us, an attraction that makes him unavoidable. We may indeed fall for him because we come to see him to be the way, the truth, and the life. We may also feel a certain discomfort: His life and his words expose the pretenses of our own. At the same time, however, we realize we are loved and forgiven and invited on a new journey for which we do not feel capable. A kind of holy helplessness prepares us to follow the One we love and trust. Love makes us vulnerable, and we give ourselves to the One for whom we have fallen, the One who made himself vulnerable.

There is another insight into following Jesus we can tease out of the phrase *falling in love*. The love God has for us and the love to which disciples of Jesus are called is a love into which we release ourselves, a love in us that lowers us out of the cloying clutches of self-aggrandizement and into the freedom of what Jesus describes as loving God with all our heart and our neighbor as ourselves (Matthew 22:37-39). Falling in love God's way is to love others without condescension, down on the level playing field of their great value as humans created in God's image. Those who love this way have allowed themselves to fall away from the pursuit of superiority fueled by insecurity and fear. They are motivated to value people for themselves and not for what they have accomplished or for what they can contribute to one's own security or success. They are falling in love. In this sense, those who have given over their lives to advancing themselves cannot really fall in love. They cannot both fall in love and love power. Loving power is treasuring what is taken or will be taken. The power to love is the power to give what has been received and will be received.

Why do we, to lesser or greater extents, search for recognition or even renown? Is this a basic human need, a drive common to us all? Or is it, rather, a symptom of deep doubt about ourselves and our worthiness? I am convinced many are driven to succeed and be recognized because they do not feel loved or accepted. They hope they will be loved because of their accomplishments and successes. They do not believe they are loved for who they are. They cannot imagine anyone falling for them apart from something they must achieve.

The person who accepts love and knows she is loved lives in a different environment. She has found a safe place where she has nothing to prove by works and everything to gain by grace. She can get on with being who she is. She cultivates an environment of personal growth and generous giving rather than self-aggrandizement. Selling herself to others is unnecessary and irrelevant. Giving herself to others is an uncompromising joy. She has fallen for them. She is in love. The only thing that makes this possible is her knowledge that someone has fallen for her where she is, rather than for what she has achieved. This is not unlike what God in Christ has done and what those with whom God has blessed our lives have also done.

Humbling ourselves before God is a phrase that appears frequently in scripture. We can interpret this humbling as a diminishing of ourselves before God, as a recognition of our unworthiness, as an admission of our failure as humans before the one in whose image we are created, and as a request for forgiveness. This interpretation is good as far as it goes, but it does not go far enough. If we stop here, humbling ourselves before God becomes a rut we get stuck in, a habitual act enabling or even encouraging our moral and spiritual dysfunction, a ritual reinforcing how utterly lost and how far removed from God we think we are. At this point it may actually dehumanize us.

The truth missing is the recognition of *God's* humbling. God falls for us. In Christ he humbles himself before us in love. This reality is expressed with eloquence and poignancy in the Apostle Paul's hymn quoted earlier. Christ, very God himself, "emptied himself by taking the form of a slave and by becoming like human beings...[and] humbled himself by becoming obedient to the point of death, even death on a cross" (Philippians 2:7-8). The God before whom we are invited to humble ourselves is the God who humbles himself before us, not to ask our forgiveness but to give us himself, to give us the strength of his love and the confidence of our true humanity. We humble ourselves before the self-humbled God so that we can discover who we really are in his image. This does lead us to a recognition and confession of our failure to be fully human; it does invite us to accept God's forgiveness. This, however, is not the main point. What is most important is that it opens a way for us to draw near to a self-humbling, loving God who both forgives our failures *and* affirms the prospect of our humanity. In other words, his love empowers us.

Empowers us for what? Empowers us to fall in love with the small. By the small, I do not mean the insignificant or trivial. I mean two things. I mean, first, those persons and that world that is close to us. And second, the small people who are marginalized by their powerlessness in the world. Scriptures give a very clear call to love and treasure the people in our close community (family, friends, fellow workers, neighbors, community of faith). They also give a very clear call to love and be advocates for those who cannot advocate for themselves and who need someone to stand and stay with them.

Families find themselves shipwrecked, businesses go under, congregations become divided because a parent, an executive, a church leader is driven toward "bigger and better things" at the expense of those who are closest to her or him. Scripture calls husband and wife to love and honor each other (Genesis 2:18-24; Ephesians 5:21-33) and to love and treasure their children (Psalm 127:3-5; Ephesians 6:4). Scripture also calls employers to treat their workers with care, consideration, and fairness (Deuteronomy 24:14-15; James 5:1-6). And church leaders are called to lead like shepherds who care for their flocks, rather than exploiting them (Ezekiel, chapter 34; I Peter 5:1-4). Love begins in the places closest to us.

Love then moves out to the neglected people and places of the world. The subversive love of God does not allow us to be satisfied with loving acts and healthy relationships within confined boundaries. It calls us to a broken world, like the world into which a boundary-breaking Christ came. John 3:16 does not say God so loved my family, my friends, my associates, my church. It says he loved the *world*; and that extravagant love has a special concern for those in the world who are most ignored or forgotten. (Proverbs 31:8-9). The first to be overlooked by most of us are the first to be the recipients of God's generosity and grace. The first to be excluded must be the first to be included (Matthew 9:10-13; 19:24; Luke 6:20; 23:39-43).

We easily overlook some people who call forth our humanity in unique ways. Consider those who come into the world with severe disabilities. No one can explain why God allows this to happen. What I do know is that the self-centered, expansionist mindset of our culture tells us to value those with exceptional physical or congitive abilities and therefore, by default, people with readily apparent disabilities are often marginalized socially and emotionally. The isolation makes it more difficult to see their humanity. I believe it also makes it more difficult for us to see *our* humanity. Our discomfort with their disability reflects our discomfort with our own disabilities, which we work hard to disguise. As we cannot know the disabled person's humanity without also coming to terms with his disability, so we cannot know our own humanity without coming to terms with *our* disabilities.

The severely disabled invite us to face our own flaws and imperfections. They discomfort us because their disability is obvious: they are dependent in a culture that idolizes independence. The discomfort reminds us of our own more-easily-hidden disabilities, which we want to deny or at least continue to keep hidden. The severely disabled expose our denials about ourselves. Threatening our illusion that we really do have it all together, they urge us to own up to our brokenness and confess our need for healing.

More important, the severely disabled person calls forth *our* humanity. It is almost impossible to take such a person for granted because the demand on our humanity, our capacity for love and understanding, threatens to pull from deep within us qualities that exceed our normalcy and give us a power only love can explain. We know that parents or caregivers who raise a severely disabled child are faced with a huge challenge. We would be foolish to feel sorry for them. The fact is, in their compassionate and persistent drive to love and care for their child and understand their child's full humanity, they often discover a far fuller measure of their own humanity. In their discovery of their capacity to love another in this way, they even learn to love themselves more fully.

Henri Nouwen, spiritual guide to tens of thousands of travelers, decided to spend the last years of his life caring for a severely mentally handicapped adult, Maurice Gould. He wanted to invest himself fully in Moe, as he was called, and help him realize and celebrate his full humanity in God's image. Nouwen knew something else, as well. He knew that by learning genuinely to love Moe, he would more deeply be discovering who Henri Nouwen was.

God invites us to fall in love with the people who sometimes make us uncomfortable because they are near us. He also invites us to fall in love with those who make us uncomfortable because they are powerless and marginalized. This is the path we travel on the way to our becoming fully human in God's image. It is not a path easily traveled. We tire, we fail, we lapse at times. This process can be discouraging, even humiliating. Sometimes we wonder why we cannot just go with the herd and look after ourselves and have some recognized success in this world. And yet, something keeps calling us back to love. Though we stumble and fall, the generous and gracious God who understands us better than we understand ourselves lifts us from our failure and says to us, "You are able to begin again."

Beginning Again

The Bible is a book of failures. The stories that populate its pages not only expose the honest mistakes of people but unmask the worst immoralities and the most blatant spiritual infidelities. The Bible begins with the story of the first humans who cannot resist the temptation to deny their very nature as humans and aspire to some greater status and recognition. This denial of our true humanity opens the way to a host of inhumanities. The story of arrogance and jealousy continues to unfold as brother murders brother, betrayal becomes common, lust drives people to abuse and exploit others, covenants are broken, and lives fall apart under the stress of impossible moral compromises.

The Old Testament is incredibly open and direct about all this, and one could get very depressed reading its stories. To be sure, there are many stories of righteous men and women who, though certainly not perfect, come across as good people who love God and their fellowmen. Often their humanity matures as they learn from their own failures and infidelities. Sometimes they begin well, only to fall to the seductions of power and lust. By the latter part of the Old Testament, however, the overall human predicament is portrayed as so hopeless that prophets begin to see and the sin-wearied begin to long for a new beginning, a future in which Israel (and the world, by implication) can return to its moorings as a people called to be humans created in the image of God, called to be free.

Fast-forward a few centuries to the New Testament. This collection of writings in different literary forms is held together by a unified message announcing a new situation: God has come into the world in the man Jesus to make it possible for us to reclaim our lost humanity. The man Jesus embodies who we are meant to be. He is the fully human human. If we become his disciples, he will show us how to recover from our brokenness and become humanly whole again.

This claim, however, is not a magic wand. Human failure does not suddenly come to an end. The euphoric intensity and subsequent transformation of the Pentecost experience in Acts 2 is not consistently sustained. Yes, there are many high moments of restored humanness where we read stories of spiritual integrity, moral strength, and extraordinary compassion. On the other hand, there are plenty of failures. The Apostle Paul's first letter to the Corinthian church describes numerous spiritual and moral transgressions within that congregation, as do other New Testament letters. The Letter of James addresses such disappointing practices as hurtful gossip and the demeaning of poor members of the Christian fellowship by the wealthy ones. There is plenty more. The New Testament, also, is a book of failures.

What, then, is the point of Jesus? Can he really enable us to reclaim our lost humanity? Does he only build up our expectations so that we can become bigger failures? We see in the New Testament church the same self-aggrandizing ploys, the same power plays, the same ethnic prejudices, the same sins, and the same failures of compassion as we did before. Is anything really different?

It is true that our capacity to violate our God-given humanity remains, and the almost two thousand years of history since the death of Jesus demonstrate the capacity has not waned. The fact is, the kingdom of God is not enforceable; love is a choice we make.

So What Is Different?

The difference is God becoming small in Jesus for his love of us. The difference is his presence and availability, then in Jesus and now in his Spirit. The difference is the concrete, living model of what it means to be fully human. The difference is Jesus' refusal to compromise his obedience to love and his willingness to pay its price: crucifixion at the hands of people too afraid to trust love. The difference is that love wins by delivering hope and overcoming death. Our capacity for sin has not changed; a new capacity for enduring love, however, has emerged and is available for those who trust it. The stubborn, faithful love so important to the Old Testament understanding of God, is now staring us in the face in

Jesus and available to us in a new way through the Spirit. The difference is the power of love, the capacity to be fully human.

Again, this does not happen by fiat. We are not made perfect; our addiction to compulsive perfectionism is not honored. Genuine love is messy; authentic love relationships are not perfect. Mistakes are made, hurts happen. People truly in love find things about their beloved they do not like; they do not live in denial. Neither do they cover their own imperfections, thereby withholding parts of themselves from the one they love. They do not make themselves likeable in order to win love; they risk themselves, flaws and all, with each other. They work with and through their differences. They trust the power of authentic love.

This is the kind of love Jesus releases in us. It is, at the same time, as free as grace and as tough as nails. It has the inviting openness of a humble heart and the unseen power of a strong wind. It risks itself because it trusts its own power. As the Apostle Paul puts it, "love never fails" (I Corinthians 13:8a). Never.

And, yes, it *is* messy. The churches of the New Testament illustrate that fact. One need only read those two letters of Paul to the Corinthian church that are included in the New Testament! Love sometimes stumbles, and then it begins again.

In a world that is always looking ahead of itself, always expecting to make clear progress, always grasping for more and better, beginning again has become a lost art. In fact, it has become a way we identify "losers": They are the ones who don't get it and have to keep starting over.

The fact is, beginning again is God's gift to us. He gives us a night of refreshment and recovery every twenty-four hours so that we can start again the next new day. He even gives us the freedom to fail, to learn from our failure, and then to try again, a little wiser. Sometimes we do not learn from our failure or blunder. We may think we were not a part of the problem, so we practice denial and deflection. There are so many others we can blame, so many other causes we can attribute. We may be living under a delusion of our own perfection, or perhaps our innocence. We may even live in denial of the possibility our motives are not pure, and then seek to diminish the hurt our blunder has caused by attributing it to a mental mistake rather than a hidden, or even a less-than-worthy motive. How many times have we tried to cover for ourselves by saying, "I didn't mean it that way," when we did? God gives us the grace to admit our mistakes and confess our sins, and the freedom to try again. That is why the Bible's insistence on not hiding our failures is good news. We can begin again.

The possibility and promise of beginning again gives us hope for our journey. Sometimes it is only a matter of seeing things differently or more clearly the next time. There is an interesting story about the Old Testament prophet Elisha, who at the time is advising the king of Israel during warfare with Aram. Aware that Elisha's good advice is enabling the Israelite army to escape the assaults of their enemy, the king of Aram decides to capture the prophet of God. Hearing that the Israelite army is camping in the town of Dothan, the king has his powerful army surround the city during the night. When the servant of Elisha wakes up and goes outside the following morning, he sees the huge Aramean army in every direction and runs to Elisha in a panic. Elisha is unperturbed. He tells his servant not to be afraid. "There are more of us than there are of them," he says. He then prays to God to open his servant's eyes. His prayer is answered. The servant looks again and sees "the mountain…full of horses and fiery chariots surrounding Elisha." The story goes on to describe a strange blindness that strikes the Aramean army, enabling Elisha to tell them they are mistaken about the location. He then leads them north to Samaria, restores their vision, and leaves them unharmed and with plenty of provisions (II Kings 6:8-23). Whatever we think of the story in terms of the details, we cannot miss the point that God sometimes invites us to take another look, especially when we seem to be facing an impossible challenge or obstacle. Sometimes what we need in order to learn from our failures is to be willing to take another look, to see in a different way.

Frequently, we refuse to see things differently. We are stuck in the rut of a closed mind or a frozen heart. We can see certain things only one way, feel about certain things one way. God invites us to look again, see differently, and trust the possibility of a different outcome.

Our pursuit of bigger and better, however, does not encourage us to begin again. There is no time for that. Admitting failure is unacceptable. We must drive forward, or we may lose what we have. Starting over is admitting we have failed. The irony is that *not* starting over guarantees a life that falls far short of its potential. Most of the attempts Abraham Lincoln made to be elected to public office were dismal failures. Each time he learned from his experience. Eventually, after running for an office political pundits thought he had no chance of winning, he was elected president of the United States. He kept starting over, and because he did, the United States was given a president who kept the country together in the face of the greatest threat to its unity and who led it out of the ugly inhumanity of slavery.

In a memorable graduation speech at Stanford University in 2005, Steve Jobs, co-founder of Apple, startled his audience by saying his firing from the company at age thirty was the best thing that could have happened to him. "The heaviness of being successful," he said, "was replaced by the lightness of being a beginner again, less sure about everything. It freed me to enter one of the most creative periods of my life" (Cohen, 2010).

Where would civilization be if we did not keep going back and beginning again? Consider, for example, scientific discoveries. They occur because dedicated scientists are willing to keep testing different new ideas, failing repeatedly, until one test proves to be a breakthrough. They learn from their failure and begin again.

Relationships prosper when we are willing to start over. Marriages and close friendships grow when failures in the relationship are admitted and fresh starts are made. I cannot count the times my wife, Keitha, and I have begun again on something until we got it right or made improvement. Sometimes it took a while, and some things we are still working on. Life is a journey of discovery if we are willing to face our muddles and missteps, and begin again.

The God of generosity and grace is the God of new beginnings. He invites us to start over. By doing so, we may take a different look at our lives and recognize that what drives us is unworthy of us. What we are pursuing could turn out to be profoundly disappointing. What we most deeply long for and hope to know could be eluding us. The honest look, the glance of integrity that exposes our compromises, is the first step toward a new beginning. The willingness to see things in a different way is the doorway to our future. God invites us to take another look.

The Bible is brimming with life-changing second looks. God tells Abram to take another look at his future, and when he does he sees a promised land. Moses takes another look at a burning bush and sees a new future of his enslaved countrymen set free. Elisha tells his servant to take another look at his hopeless situation and see good news. A fugitive in the wilderness named David sees beyond his desperate state and, hope against hope, sees an unimaginable future of influence. The prophet Hosea looks at his broken marriage, and with his God-given capacity for second looks he sees restoration. The Apostle Paul has to be blinded to be able to take a second look. Whereas he has seen these humble, uneducated disciples of Jesus as an insidious threat to his traditional faith, he now comes to a fear-free second look and sees them as witnesses to a new fulfillment of that faith. The Apostle Peter has to take many second looks at his own lack of trust in the gospel's inclusiveness, and each time begins again. The second look often leads us to a new beginning or a chance for another and better try, another and better way.

The God of generosity and grace waits patiently and lovingly for those who are willing to take a fresh look and begin again. He bestows upon us the gift of a certain unsettledness. He lovingly plagues us with a bothering suspicion that our old dreams are demeaning to ourselves and others, a sellout of our humanity, a sadness to the God who created us in his image. Then God calls us to begin again with a better vision of our humanity, in his image. Our new beginning may be a modest step, like treating a son or a daughter with more trust. Or it may be a huge step, like a complete change in the direction of our lives. In either case our new beginning is a decision to go in another direction or take a risk on something unknown or on something at which we have previously failed. It is a decision to do certain things and not others. It means drawing a line, separating our course of action from lesser ways. It means taking sides.

Taking Sides

The idea of taking sides may sound narrow-minded. We side with a sports team for geographical, historical, cultural, emotional, and various other reasons. I become very close-minded and emotionally immature when I sit in front of the TV and watch my alma mater play a college football game. My judgment is one-sided; I passionately wish my team to win, which of course requires the other team to lose. Taking sides, as we most often use the term, implies a contest or fight of some kind, with only one party winning. It requires a loser.

If only my side could win without the other side losing. I love it when my team wins—and I hate it. I hate it because I usually feel badly for the losing team. I remember when my college football team won its first national championship. I was euphoric because the opposing team, an established national powerhouse, was highly favored to win, and my team was almost universally looked upon as an upstart from nowhere who did not even deserve to be in the national championship game. My elation came from my identification with the underdogs, who at the conclusion of the game miraculously found themselves elevated to the position of top dogs.

It did not take long, however, for the elation to be disturbed by sadness. When I picked up the phone and called my friend Bill for a celebratory conversation we shared a brief cheer for our school and team. Then Bill's voice quieted, and speaking of the coach of the losing team, he said, "He is a decent man." With my eyes still on the TV, I saw the camera capture the dejection and grief of the players on the losing team, and the lone, dignified profile of their coach. Bill had called me to the other side. It was not enough that I stay on my side

I suspect that nagging discomfort with winning at the expense of the losers comes from the heart of our humanity. There is something in us that, if we allow ourselves to feel it, does not allow us to gloat when we win and someone else loses. When a winning team feels it, they have the grace and compassion to give attention to their losing opponent, to confront them with sensitivity and comfort them with understanding. I imagine that in those moments God smiles.

The ability and willingness to side with the other, the one who is not us and shares a different experience from ours, is God's gift, when it is not an act of self-protection or self-aggrandizement. Sometimes we take someone's side not to identify with them or share their burden but to advantage ourselves through them. We understand well the strategy of siding with another for our own benefit. International diplomacy does just that. Political campaigns are built on convincing as many groups as possible that the candidate is on their side. Advertising is premised on convincing as many people as possible that the company offering a certain product really has their interest at heart, whereas we all know the company's interest in selling as much as possible is their compelling motivation. None of this is disinterested charity. It is the art of international diplomacy, the secret to effective political campaigns, the strategy of successful advertising. It is not the exercise of God's gift of compassion. It is entering the world of the other for gaining strength and position.

We need not belittle such activity. It is simply the way our less-than-perfect world does business. Nor do we have any right to criticize others simply for being a part of it. Many of them are people of character who live compassionately. Furthermore, all of us are quite capable of using other people and groups solely for our own profit. Any of us, no matter how noble and unselfish our pursuits seem to be, can be insidious self-seekers. We do, however, need to say there is a very different kind of siding with another person or group. Instead of our making a self-serving claim on them, we recognize and accept their claim on us. We see them not in terms of a possible advantage but as part of our diverse family. We see a common humanity.

Recognizing and accepting others' claim on us most definitively plays out in the relationship between the advantaged and the disadvantaged. If you are reading this book, you are most likely among the advantaged. You may not have a sizeable investment portfolio, but in comparison to the truly disadvantaged people of our society, you are advantaged. For those who claim to be followers of Jesus, as well as those who are considering taking that step, what cannot be ignored and what must be faced squarely is the fact that Jesus invites us to lower ourselves, to become small in order to enter the world of the disadvantaged, as he did. This is the place where Jesus must be found, wherever else we find him. "I assure you that when you have done it for one of the least of these brothers and sisters of mine," he says, "you have done it for me" (Matthew 25:40b). Jesus not only taught it, he lived it. Had you lived in Palestine in the early part of the first century CE and wanted to find Jesus during his three-year mission, you would most likely have found him among the poorest and most disreputable.

The simple truth is this: Those who do not humble themselves do not find God. This is not debasement, putting ourselves down so as to make God seem so much higher than we. It is dis-

covery, finding how close he is to us. He is present most definitively in those who have the least and are considered the least. A
wise old rabbi was once asked why it was so few people seemed to
be finding God. He replied that not many people were willing to
look that low.

I am convinced that taking sides with the least of these is one
of the most ignored, if not *the* most ignored, invitation of Jesus to
those who would be his disciples. How could a reader of both Old
and New Testaments miss it? How could so many remake Christianity into a religion for the advantaged? How could Jesus become
the god who blesses our obsessive pursuit of the American Dream?
How could so many advantaged Christians be content with giving a contribution for missions but not carry the poor in their
hearts? And how could so many disadvantaged Christians carry
deep resentment in their hearts because they expected Jesus to
do a better job at prospering them—the Jesus who himself had
"no place to lay his head"! (Matthew 8:20b). How does it happen
that the faith of the lowly Nazarene becomes confiscated and corrupted by a culture of bigger and better, for myself?

I imagine what happens is that, at some level, we know or
sense that the life and message of Jesus have no room to include
our selfish pursuits and worldly ambitions. And if, unwilling to
surrender those socially acceptable drives, we at the same time
want to acquire some semblance of a Christian spirituality, we
settle on a proper, civilized Christian religion, with no demands
that would disturb our lifestyle. We reinterpret Jesus' radical message of finding God in the lowest place and in the marginalized
person into the message of finding God in the private, protected
world of our successes and structures. We must also choose to ignore the recurring message of Old Testament seers, stated with
unusually powerful eloquence by Isaiah:

If you remove the yoke from among you,
the finger-pointing, the wicked speech;

> if you open your heart to the hungry,
>   and provide abundantly
> for those who are afflicted,
>   your light will shine in the darkness,
>   and your gloom will be like the noon.
> Isaiah 58:9b-10

We can reconstruct Jesus by making him an idol we manipulate for ourselves, or we can see him as an icon inviting us to follow him into the lives of the least. Jesus calls us to lower ourselves and side with the poor and the outcast. He beckons us to follow him and cross over to the side of those who are outside the boundaries of the socially and materially successful. He leads us to the other side, outside the mainstream, to where there is no advantage to be found, and a life to be gained.

I have profound admiration for Dorothy Jones. An ordained minister, she forsook the comfort and security of her America and took sides with India. For most of her adult life she cared for impoverished orphans in that country. One of the places where she served was the Salvation Army's Sion Children's Home in Mumbai (Bombay). While she was there, an unmarried woman left her baby at the doorstep of the home. Dorothy took him in and cared for him as long as she served in that home, and later at another home for older boys where he was transferred. Suresh, now nearly fifty, was that baby and calls Dorothy "my first American mother." (There was a second American mother, Alice Stiles, whom I did not know, who also cared for Suresh in his latter childhood years.) Dorothy, who passed away a few years ago, was not an imposing figure. She preferred the background. Most of the people who knew her in the United States knew little about her life and legacy in India, and she seemed surprisingly content about that.

Suresh Pawar, however, does know. Dorothy Jones *chose* to become his mother, *chose* to side with an orphaned baby, one of

God's "least of these." One of the many things Suresh learned from his first and second American mothers was to choose sides with the disadvantaged and help them discover their God-given humanity. He has given his own life to ministry among the lower classes of his country. In the early years of the AIDS epidemic in India, Suresh trained teams to help families affected by the disease to cope and give care to their stricken family member.

Dorothy, Alice, and Suresh sided with the disadvantaged. One generation showed the next generation how to choose the side of the marginalized. I happen to know Suresh's son Ashish, and he is doing the same with his young life.

Dorothy, Alice, Suresh, and Ashish are living embodiments of the life to which God calls us all. They teach us to find life by losing it. They demonstrate that love is true when the lover accepts the claims of the other on his life. They prove the power of becoming small. And their lives are an invitation to us all to discover the freedom of lowering ourselves.

One of the great paradoxes of Jesus' life is that he offers us abundant life (John 10:10b) while also inviting us to lose our lives (Mark 8:34-35). He says we can find fulfillment if we empty ourselves. In these pages we have attempted to show how essential this supreme paradox is to realizing our true humanity in God's image. What remains for us now is to claim the moments of our lives—or better, to allow the moments to claim us. What remains is for us to learn how to live the day.

Living the Day

When you think about it, it is remarkable how much denial we tolerate. We deny all kinds of things so as not to let them stand in the way we are currently going. We deny our hunger for close relationships because they can be demanding and even messy, and we need to get on with our important work. We deny our desire for more depth in life because we do not want to face the emptiness of our unexamined lives. We deny the duplicity of our compromises because we are convinced our success requires them. We resist letting ourselves feel our starvation for meaning, for love, for God. We deny what cries out from our souls *today*, the cry to stop for a few moments and notice someone, even notice our own selves, notice a still small voice that may be God. And what we hear over our denials may sound something like: "Live this day. It will soon be gone. You have only so many of them, and you don't even know how many." And here we have the truth that threatens all our denials: We will all die.

A long time ago, Samuel Johnson and his biographer Boswell were having a conversation about death. Boswell said something to the effect that death was a most unpleasant subject, to which Johnson replied, "So much so, sir, that all of life is but keeping away the thought of it" (Boswell, 1791). In Johnson's day death came earlier. In our day, a longer life span encourages us all the more to postpone the thoughts of the inevitable. Our ambitions are so large, our dreams so demanding, our drivenness so unrelenting, we cannot allow ourselves to consider there may not be time to finish all we imagine. Or worse, an unfortunate accident may bring an early end to our earthly striving. So we live in denial, helped by a no-end-to-life culture dedicated to hiding death as much as possible.

In contrast to our culture's denial, the Bible is almost brutally confrontational about death. The psalmist reminds us our "days go by like a shadow" (Psalm 144:4). Such words do not inspire us to make big plans. Instead, they inspire us to "number our days" (Psalm 90:12), to treasure what we have as well as what may yet come, God willing. The certainty of our eventual death paired with the uncertainty of its timing invite us to live the day.

The author of Psalm 84 was most likely a Levite priest who, for reasons we do not know, finds himself unable to serve in, or even enter, the temple in Jerusalem. This exclusion is, for him, not unlike death. His forced exile keeps him from the best days of his life. He envies even the sparrows and swallows that are still able to nest and raise their young near the sacred altar where he once served as a priest and surely had moments when he felt the Divine touch his heart. "Better is a single day in your courtyards," he writes, "than a thousand days anywhere else!" (Psalm 84:10a). He wishes he had it to do over again. Perhaps he wishes he had appreciated it more at the time. Perhaps he even wishes he had done better.

We may know the feeling: "I wish I had some of those days with my kids to do over again; wish I had more fully realized what a treasure they were." Or, "I wish I had said what was on my heart to my mom or dad before they passed on. To whom do I say it now?" And, "I wish I had listened, *really* listened, better to my friend; wish I had been able to get over my discomfort with his discomfort and somehow be with him during his suffering." "I wish I had some of those days back."

The days pass and we sometimes fail to seize them because we are always looking ahead, expecting a better and less inconvenient opportunity. Or maybe we just do not want to stop and seize that day because we have these bigger plans to carry out. And the day comes when we realize we missed some of the rich opportunities to live those days well. We let them slip through our too busy, or perhaps paralyzed, fingers. We see that our days really *are* numbered. The psalmist says to pay attention to each of them because they disappear "like a fleeting shadow" (Psalm 144:4 NIV).

If asked about death, few of us would deny the reality of it, nor deny our days are limited. But knowing this fact is one thing, and living with it is another. There is plenty to help us ignore it. We can avoid the thoughts of our mortality by keeping busy. We can even get ourselves so distracted we can almost pretend death will not really happen to *us*. During the last days of William Saroyan's life, when it was clear he was dying, the famous dramatist and writer commented: "I always knew everyone had to die sooner or later. I just thought an exception would be made in my case."

Some of us are uncomfortable talking about death. Death puts a definite limit on life's possibilities. Thinking about death puts a damper on the future.

Or does it?

Convince me I am going to die some day, and I may just make the most of the time I have. I may just see the day as an opportunity to find love, discover grace, and live in hope. I may begin to fall in love with the God who lowers himself to enter my day and meet me there. I may even learn to love myself as a unique person created in God's image who has been given this particular day to discover and live this authentic human life. I may even love others this particular day, as Jesus did each day of his thirty-three years. No one can rob me of *this* day. Life is short. I can choose to live this day.

The denial of death may live within every denial that stunts me. If I deny my death I can breeze through these days as if they will never come to an end. If I deny my death I can say I will love myself, or others, or God, some other time. If I deny my death I can indefinitely postpone becoming who I am in God's image.

God invites us to stop denying our death so we can start living. Accept that we are dust and to dust we will return (Genesis 3:19c). Live well the days he gives us. Let the days of blessing encourage us, the days of curse deepen us. Once we abandon our strategies of postponement, once we start living in the now—what II Corinthians 6:2 calls "the right time" that is "the day of salvation"—we are moving away from our illusions about the future and embracing the promise and grace of this day. We are receiving God's gift of today.

The surprising truth is, this is how we best sort out our future. The future of someone who is not living the day is a future for which he is not prepared. The good news Jesus announces is that the kingdom of God is *here*. We can enter it, live it, *today*. Jesus' message gives us plenty of clues about how we can do that.

(Check out his Sermon on the Mount, recorded in Matthew 5–7, for starters.) And there is more than enough in the entire Bible to keep us working on living for the rest of our lives—not to mention eternity. Jesus invites us to live today as if the future has come, to practice the future this day, and to get better at it each day.

We will probably never get it perfectly right in this life. There is always more to learn, practice, and master. Without fail, the people I know who have the greatest spiritual depth also have a remarkably genuine humility about themselves; they are the people most honest about their imperfections and failings. This frees them, I think, to live the day more fully because they recognize there is something new to learn and become. They teach us to live the day well because they approach the day with the modesty of a genuine seeker. They become small.

Becoming Small

So we return to the invitation we have been extending for the course of this book. Risk becoming small. Treasure small things, small moments, small matters. Face the day as it so sufficiently is, and not as we wish it to be or might try to force it to become. Love those near us and those on the vulnerable edges for who they are and not for how we imagine them to be in our schemes or dismiss them to be from our narrow perspective. Be genuinely present with those God brings into our lives, or even into just one of our days. Come out from behind our self-protective ruses and trust the integrity of who we are in God's image. Recognize and confess our lives are too bloated, too distracted; our hopes too self-serving; our gains too short-lived and shallow; the hunger of our hearts too unsatisfied. Begin again by becoming small.

Becoming small is how we find our soul, our true self. This is true for all of us, no matter what our station or stature in the world. Bernard of Clairvaux is reputed to have said, "If you are to do the work of a prophet, what you need is not a scepter but a hoe." If you want to be a CEO, spend quality time with those at the "lowest levels" of your company, and do not stop doing it. If you want to be a respected teacher, never stop being a know-nothing learner. If you want to be a really helpful counselor, do not think or pretend you have all the answers. If you want to be a follower of Jesus, know you have to begin again each day with the simple basics and with deep humility. Begin small, stay small. If we lose the small things, the big things will prove empty. We change the world for good when we begin with ourselves and our own relationships. My prayers for world peace, for example, invite me to ask first if *I* am at peace and if *I* am making peace in my own small sphere of life where I have the potential for significant influence for good. I must seek to live well in my small world if I am to do my best for the larger. None of us is called to be larger than life. We are only called to live our own lives well at whatever ground level we find ourselves.

The truth is, small people can release enormous, life-changing power in their small places and even beyond. At the time of this writing, revolutions against political oppression are taking place across northern Africa and in the Middle East. The discontent feeding these events has been brewing for many years, but the event that sparked the fires of unrelenting protest was the action of one small person in a relatively insignificant town in Tunisia. The person was an unemployed street vendor who set himself on fire to protest against the government that exploited the poorer classes of that country. One small person, one small moment, and the course of that part of the world is radically altered and the effects are felt around the world. The courageous act of a "power-less" man sparks hope for one nation after another.

A story in the Old Testament has some similarities to this

one. King Saul, corrupted and diminished by the power through which he now defines himself, appeals to the same lust for power to motivate his officials against David. Ahimelech the priest is brought before Saul and pressured to betray David. He is clearly in a powerless position. Saul can do with him as he pleases. Instead of playing up to Saul, however, he speaks truth to power and calls Saul to account for his unfairness and evil intent toward David. Ahimelech is the one without power, and he pays with his life. It is *his* cause, however, that wins out. Saul's is lost (See I Samuel 22:6-19).

The Bible tells us story after story about the power of small in the face of arrogant power. There is a teenage shepherd called David who slays a behemoth of a man called Goliath with a slingshot and a few stones. There is Gideon, leader of Israel, who is told by God to cut down the size of his army from thirty thousand to three hundred, so that the Midianites would know they were not defeated by superior military strength but by God. There is a prophet called Jeremiah who is kicked around, abused, thrown in prison, and as powerless as a lone prophet can be, yet the truth and power of his words prevail. We must also mention the Apostle Paul, who traveled the Mediterranean world alone or with an apostle-in-training or two, making a few tents along the way to earn a meager living; preaching a message that seemed to insult most who heard it; maligned, beaten, imprisoned, and thrown out of town on more than one occasion; escaping with his life only because he was a protected Roman citizen; and living the last days of his life we know not where. From the information we have, he did not look like much, and admitted it. On the other hand, he just happened to be the apostle of the Christian faith who risked his life on the absolute inclusiveness of Jesus' message and mission. It is beyond explaining This unimposing but stubborn man kept plodding from place to place, from one ethnicity to another, offending some and convincing others, misunderstood even by many of his own converts. Why? He intends to build a huge bridge from an ethnic Christian faith to a world Christian faith. He changed the world.

Ahimelech, David, Gideon, Jeremiah, and Paul risk small-ness, as have countless others who have put their lives on the line for truth or love. They become underdogs, trusting what we might call a counter-intuitive strength. It is the strength of courageous weakness in the face of power. It comes to any of us when we dis-cover there is action worth taking, a witness worth giving, even when no backup is available.

I saw an interesting study of bullying among teens in an in-depth TV documentary program recently. A number of scenarios were set up, with hidden cameras, where volunteers were placed in a situation where they were led to believe was an opportunity to develop certain skills or competencies. Also placed into the situation were two scripted actors—one, the leader and instructor scripted to bully, and the other, the person to be bullied. The real volunteers had no idea these two were actors.

As the bullying progressed, I could sense the discomfort of the volunteers. I wondered why they would put up with the bullying as long as they did. (It is so easy for someone on the sidelines to express indignation in such a case, when *they* are observing safely from the sidelines.) In every case in the ongoing experiment, one of the volunteers finally stepped forward to protest the bullying. Interestingly, once he or she did stand up for the bullied individ-ual, the other volunteers felt free to express their own discomfort and side with the victim. One person crosses the line to the other side, risks standing with the one who is being bullied. One person trusts his or her own humanity and in doing so gives confidence to his or her peers to trust their own. One person enters the world of the person made small by the powerful and has the courage to stand with him. One person becomes small as well, and subjects him or herself to the possibility of suffering at the hands of power (the authority-figure bully). Which, come to think of it, is some-thing like what Jesus did.

In fact, Jesus invites us to do the same thing.

The Old Testament prophets, the gospel of Jesus, and the New Testament writers all teach us to side with those who are treated as small. We cannot side with them, however, without becoming like them. As they are the ones who are vulnerable and powerless, so we become vulnerable and powerless. We come out from behind the security of our office, the power of our position, the protectiveness of the institutions with which we are identified. We risk alienating associates, neighbors, and even family. We stand with those with whom Jesus stood. We become small.

This is not a call to large-scale social revolution, which often results in repression of a different sort. It is a call to personal courage where we each refuse to keep our distance, refuse to overlook the overlooked, and refuse to justify our smug comfort. It is a call to claim the better part of who we are by getting beyond the fear that confines and weakens us. It is a call to shed the thick exterior of who we pretend to be and risk the compassionate center of who Jesus says, with him, we *truly* are.

This core of ourselves is, indeed, a seemingly small thing. It has no worldly power, only a spiritual power that may come across as irrational at times—irrational because we cannot formulate, calculate, or calibrate how it works. We only know those who act from this core trust its power so thoroughly they take big risks. Risks such as the ones taken by the inhabitants of a small French village during Nazi occupation who practiced a conspiracy of silence by hiding Jews and refusing to divulge their brave secret. Or the risk could be the one taken by a corporate executive who refuses to maximize shareholder profits by keeping the wages of workers too low to support a reasonable cost of living, or who, in refusing to bypass safety standards for greater company profits, puts his own position in jeopardy. Or, the risk could be taken by the pastor of a congregation who so believes the gospel that she challenges a self-absorbed congregation to lose their lives, advocate for the marginalized in their community, and transform their congregation into a genuinely inclusive family. Whoever we may be, living authentically in God's image is a risk, because it is a rejection of the self-serving drives that enthrall us and keep us afraid to put our integrity on the line and release our compassion.

There is a clear choice before us every day, whether we are just beginning our spiritual journey or have been on it a long time. The choice is whether on this day to be full of ourselves or to have fullness of life. We lean toward self-fullness when we ask, "What's in it for me?" If we allow that question to possess us, we have chosen the self-interested mindset of protective religion over the spiritual journey of faith. The prophet Malachi exposes the motivation perfectly: "Serving God is useless. What do we gain by keeping his obligation?" (Malachi 3:14 NRSV). What, indeed. All we may gain is our souls.

An old, well-known hymn of Washington Gladden is still found in many Christian hymnals. It is a prayer of unambitious ambition. It is a deeply serious prayer for strength to do the all-important small things. Things like sharing a winning word of love with someone who is in a dark place; coming alongside someone who is losing his way and helping him find his way home. It is also a prayer for patience in an impatient society, for simple trust and strong hope in a world of unfulfilled dreams and doomed schemes. Written in the Victorian language of the late nineteenth century, the hymn still speaks truth. The opening lines sum up the prayer: "O Master, let me walk with thee in lowly paths of service free. " Free, indeed.

The lowly paths are truly the most ambitious because they ask us to make the toughest choices. They require us to make sacrifices for good and not gain. They call forth from us the courage to let go of the lesser ambitions of self-advancement for the greater ambitions of God's kingdom of grace, generosity, and compassion. They invite us to become big enough to become small, whatever our place in the social strata. There we will find the treasure, there the meaning of our humanity, there the real fullness of life.

Pat-Pat

That's what the children called her. She was in the latter years of middle age. An earlier stroke had left her face partially paralyzed, and her head and upper torso tilted to the side. Her speech was rapid and garbled, and I couldn't understand most of what she said. Some thought she was mentally challenged. A few adults probably considered her "an unfortunate person."

There were some, however, who knew better, in particular the children in our church nursery and the homeless men and women whom she helped to feed and clothe. They loved Pat-Pat, and it seemed they had the ability to understand what she was saying. I personally observed my four-year-old grandson's deep affection for Pat-Pat when he entered the church building on a Sunday morning and spotted her. She would send the sound of his name across the room like a love letter, and Ben would light up and run into her arms.

Pat-Pat and Ben became prayer partners. They prayed for each other. Our daughter Heather said, "When you get on Ben's prayer list, you receive multiple prayers. He prays for you in the morning, at mealtimes, and before bed...and his prayers go on and on. He is quite dramatic and charismatic!"

That year Pat-Pat suffered a massive stroke. As she lay near death in the hospital for a few days, Ben faithfully prayed for her to get better. He believed God answered prayer, and his vigil was diligent.

Pat-Pat lingered for a week or so in the critical-care unit, and Ben continued to pray. He claimed healing for her. She finally slipped away.

Heather was faced with the difficult task of breaking the news to Ben. She tenderly took him aside and told him what had happened. Ben did not take it well. He refused to accept what he was hearing. His four-year-old mind could not grasp that a fervent prayer like his could fail. He lashed out: "Why are you telling me this! This makes me so very, very sad. I'm disappointed! Well, this is not true. She is going to be here on Sunday and is going to rock me in the nursery. You'll see. I prayed for her to get better and she did."

Heather told Ben it was okay to feel sad and mad and disappointed. People feel like this when someone they love dies. She talked about how sometimes Jesus answers our prayers in ways that are different from what we hoped for. They talked about how Pat-Pat was in heaven talking and laughing with Jesus and that she wasn't sick or hurting anymore. The next day Ben asked how it was that Pat-Pat wasn't sick anymore, so Heather talked about her new body in heaven. Ben became very fascinated about Pat-Pat's new body.

"Well," he said, "what does she look like now?"

"Good question," said Heather. "Why don't you draw me a picture of Pat-Pat in heaven."

Ben began to draw, and then he called Heather over. "Can you help me draw her glasses? I don't know how."

"Sure, Ben, but do you think she needs glasses in heaven?"

"Yes, she wouldn't look right without them." Heather drew the glasses. Nothing was going to rob Pat-Pat of her full identity, nor Ben of the details of her memory.

Then Heather noticed Ben had drawn a number of lines around Pat-Pat. She asked Ben what the lines were. Ben knew exactly what he meant by them. He explained: "They're all the babies and the children lining up to sit on Pat-Pat's lap so she can rock them. That is her job in heaven." As the day went on, Ben added more and more babies to the line and then he eventually told Heather that he had to draw a road to get to her. "Wow," said Heather, "that's a lot of babies."

"Well, she can handle it, Mom," Ben answered.

Ben saw it true. His child eyes had claimed the beauty and significance in a life sufficiently humble and meek for few to notice, save those with eyes to see compassion without pretense.

Pat-Pat's life is a sign and a lesson for me. It teaches me that enduring significance is not found in our achievements; it is found in the countless small ways we value and touch people—those close to us and those considered the least of these. It is not found in the size of our estate, or the level of our social status, or the volume of our cheering crowds; it is found in genuine humility and self-emptying compassion. It is not even found in the size of our charity; it is found in the genuineness of our caring. I would like to be able to look back on my own life and treasure the times I was willing to be sufficiently human to love deeply those close to me and reach out to others I would not otherwise touch. Perhaps you long for the same.

This, I believe, is where and how we find the genuine beauty God gives our lives, the beauty of small, the humble glamour of giving ourselves to another, the stunning appeal of a child who can't wait to be nestled on Pat-Pat's lap, where God is present and where the child sees Jesus—perhaps with glasses on.

God places us all near people to be loved and to love us and he says, "Take the risk." And he positions us to reach out beyond our inner circle to the larger circle of the "other," and he says, "Take the risk. Share yourself generously, keep little for yourself . . . until you are small enough to make a difference that really matters. In that person, that place, that matter, that moment, you will find me. And finding me, you will find life."

Works Cited

Bonhoeffer, Dietrich. 1953. *Letters and Papers from Prison*. London: SCM Press.

Boswell, James. 1791. *The Life of Samuel Johnson*. London: Penguin Books.

Cohen, William D. "The Power of Failure." *The New York Times*. November 27, 2010, p. A15.

Dillard, Annie. 1982. *Teaching a Stone to Talk*. New York: Harper & Row.

Frost, Robert. 1969. "The Oven Bird." In *The Poetry of Robert Frost: The Collected Poems*. Edited by Edward Connery Lathem. New York: Henry Holt and Company.

Howe, Reuel. 1953. *Man's Need and God's Action*. New York: The Seabury Press.

Loder, James E. 1981. *The Transforming Moment: Understanding Convictional Experiences*. San Francisco: Harper & Row.

Lukovich, Mike. Cartoon in *The Atlanta Journal-Constitution*, April 18, 2011, p. A18.

MacCulloch, Diarmaid. 2010. *Christianity: The First Three Thousand Years*. New York: Viking Penguin.

McLaren, Brian. 2004. *A Generous Orthodoxy*. Grand Rapids: Zondervan.

Moore, Margaret. An untitled poem published in *The Officer*. The Salvation Army: August 1969, 536.

Needleman, Jacob. 2007. *Why Can't We Be Good?* New York: Jeremy P. Tarcher/ Penguin.

Norris, Kathleen. 2008. *Acedia: A Marriage, Monks, and a Writer's Life*. New York: Riverhead Books.

Nouwen, Henri. 2004. *Eternal Seasons*. Edited by Michael Ford. Notre Dame: Ave Maria Press.

Weis, Othmar, and Joseph Alois Daisenberger. 2010. *Passionsspiele Oberammergau*. Edited by Christian Stuckl and Otto Hube. Translated by Ingrid Shafer. Oberammergau, Germany: Gemeinde Oberammergau.

Pagitt, Doug. 2008. *A Christianity Worth Believing: Hope-Filled, Open-Armed, Alive-and-Well Faith for the Left Out, Left Behind, and Let Down in Us All*. San Francisco: Jossey-Bass.

Pennington-Russell. "Lessons from Stone Mountain" (guest column), *The Atlanta Journal-Constitution*, January 9, 2011, p. A21

Rodriguez, Richard. "Future Shock: The Bigger We Feel, the Smaller We Want to Be." *The Los Angeles Times*. January 2, 2000, M1.

Shulevitz, Judith. "Time and Possibilities," review of *In the Valley of the Shadow* by James L. Kugel. New York: *Free Press*, February 13, 2011.

Smith, Betty. 1943. *A Tree Grows in Brooklyn*. Pleasantdale, NY, and Montreal: The Reader's Digest Association, Inc.

Van Wyck, Brooks. 1879. "Letter to Brandes," in *The Ordeal of Mark Twain*. New York: E. P. Dutton and Company.